CRITICAL ACCLAIM FOR AI

"Having edited the volume *Atomic Ghost: Poets F[...]*ing read a great deal of poetry on Hiroshim[...]hibakusha, I find Yasusada's 'Mad Daughter and Big-Bang' simply [...]moving and revealing poems ever written on the effects of the Bomb. If we ignore the strange and wonderful writing we find in this book, future readers may judge the real fraud not Yasusada, but us. "　　　　　　　　　　　—John Bradley

"(The Yasusada author) has done a brilliant job in inventing a world at once ritualized and yet startlingly modern, timeless yet documentary, archaicized yet *au courant*—a poetic world that satisfies our hunger for the authentic, even though that authentic world is itself a perfect simulacrum. . . . Like Pound's *Homage to Sextus Propertius*, the Yasusada notebooks force us to go back to the 'originals,' so as to see what they really were and how they have been transformed."
　—Marjorie Perloff, Professor of Comparative Literature, Stanford University

"(It is) a mistake, I think, in having 'Kent Johnson' stand for the author. He/She/They should be known as the Yasusada Author, much as we refer to a Renaissance painter as the Master of the X Altar.. . . (Yasusada) is both the greatest poet of Hiroshima and its most unreliable witness."
　　　　　　　　　　—Eliot Weinberger, *Boston Review* & *The Village Voice*

"Here, a pseudonymous writer rises from the actual site of flash-point and passes into the hailstones of injunction and constraint—someone plying a clenched intensity and open parentheses who has poised the mind to risk that very failure which yields actual poetry. No aboutness about it."　　　　　—C.D. Wright

"Yasusada's manuscripts have attracted wide attention. Among the readers is included a poet who confessed that he was so moved that he "could not sleep." . . . Whether Yasusada's fictional texts are worth appraisal as that which expresses a desire for a union with the victims of the atomic bombs, or whether they are a beautiful but superficial composition which evades the issues of responsibility and guilt, one cannot find any sort of agreement among poets and critics in American circles. . . . In the wariness not unlike that of evading a taboo, one might feel an inarticulate pressure against this issue which seems to be lurking in the American society. Now that Yasusada's fictionality is admitted, the ripples of this scandal will reach further. One could not overlook then how the discussion will develop, particularly on the relation between the responsibility and guilt over the atomic bombs and the way literary fiction should pose itself in opposition to these heavy questions."　　　　　　　—Akitoshi Nagahata, *Asahi Shimbun*

Doubled Flowering:
From the Notebooks of Araki Yasusada

The poet Araki Yasusada

Doubled Flowering:
From the Notebooks of Araki Yasusada

Edited and Translated by Tosa Motokiyu,
Ojiu Norinaga, and Okura Kyojin

ROOF BOOKS
NEW YORK

ISBN: 0-937804-71-1
Library of Congress Catalog Card No.: 97-069741

ACKNOWLEDGEMENTS

The Abiko Quarterly with James Joyce Studies (Japan), *Aerial, The American Poetry Review, The Asahi Shimbun* (Japan), *Atomic Ghost: Poems of the Nuclear Age* (Coffee House Press), *Boston Review, BullHead, Conjunctions, Countermeasures, Denver Quarterly, First Intensity, Grand Street, Heat* (Australia), *Il Nuovo Giornale dei Poeti* (Italy), *Ironwood, The Manchester Guardian* (England), *Mike and Dale's Younger Poets, Lateral* (Spain), *Lo Straniero* (Italy), *London Magazine* (England), *Novoe Literaturnoe Obozrenie* (Russia), *Poetry Review* (England), *Stand* (England), *The Sydney Morning Herald* (Australia), *Witz, The Village Voice, Vuelta* (Mexico), and the chapbooks, *Joyous Young Pines* (Juniper Press), and *Sentences for Jack Spicer Renga* (Bloody Twin Press).

Thanks to Marc Welch for assistance with computer layout.
Special gratitude to Katsumi Takahashi, Keiko Takahashi, and Sanae Takahashi.

Design by Deborah Thomas.

This book was made possible, in part, by a grant from the New York State Council on the Arts.

Roof Books are published by
Segue Foundation
303 East 8th Street
New York, New York 10009

In this novel before me there is a painting in a book the protagonist is reading, in which a woman holds a mirror. Behind the reflection of her face is the reflection of a mountain, made tiny by the distance. I wonder what she could be thinking, thinks the protagonist, looking up from the book. I wonder what is happening on the hidden face of that mountain in the mirror . . .

Araki Yasusada

[Undated entry, in looseleaf, found inserted into a copy of Origuchi Shinobu's Book of the Dead.*]*

Contents

Introducing Araki Yasusada
(and Ozaki Kusatao and Akutagawa Fusei)

The notebooks of the Hiroshima poet Araki Yasusada were discovered by his son in 1980, eight years following the poet's death. The manuscripts comprise fourteen spiral notebooks whose pages are filled with poems, drafts, English class assignments, diary entries, recordings of Zen dokusan encounters and other matter. In addition, the notebooks are interleaved with hundreds of insertions, including drawings, received correspondence, and carbon copies of the poet's letters.

Although Yasusada was active in important avant-garde groups such as Ogiwara Seisensui's *Soun (Layered Clouds)* and the experimental renga circle *Kai (Oars)* and was an acquaintance of several well-known writers and artists like Taneda Santoka, Ozaki Hosai, Kusano Shimpei, and Shiryu Morita, his work, along with that of his renga collaborators Ozaki Kusatao and Akutagawa Fusei, is virtually unknown. But the writing found in Yasusada's manuscripts is fascinating for its biographical disclosure, formal diversity, and linguistic elan. Much of the experimental impetus, interestingly, comes from Yasusada's encounter in the mid-1960's with the poetry of the American Jack Spicer and the French critic Roland Barthes: Yasusada had fluency in English and French, and there are numerous quotes from, or references to, both of these literary figures in the later work. The notebooks reveal, in fact, that Yasusada was undertaking a work parallel to Spicer's letters and "translations" in *After Lorca*, to be entitled *After Spicer*.

Yasusada was born in 1907 in the city of Kyoto, where he lived until 1921, when his family moved to Hiroshima. He attended Hiroshima University sporadically between 1925 and 1928, with the intent of receiving a degree in Western Literature. Due, however, to his Father's illness, he was forced, in the interests of the family, to undertake full-time employment with the postal service and withdraw from his formal studies.

In 1930 he married his only wife Nomura, with whom he had two daughters and a son. In 1936, Yasusada was conscripted into the Japanese Imperial Army and worked as a clerk in the Hiroshima division of the Military Postal Service. His wife and youngest daughter, Chieko, died instantly in the atomic blast on August 6. His daughter Akiko survived, yet perished less than four years later from radiation sickness. His son, Yasunari, an infant at the time, was with relatives outside the city.

Yasusada died in 1972 after a long struggle with cancer. Akutagawa Fusei died of similar cause in 1971. The fate of Ozaki Kusatao is unknown to us.

We have generally arranged dated material chronologically, except where thematic considerations have led us to do otherwise. Undated material has been sequenced according to our best judgement.

—*Tosa Motokiyu, Ojiu Norinaga, Okura Kyojin.*

MAD DAUGHTER AND BIG-BANG
December 25, 1945*

Walking in the vegetable patch
late at night, I was startled to find
the severed head of my
mad daughter lying on the ground.

Her eyes were upturned, gazing at me, ecstatic-like...

(From a distance it had appeared
to be a stone, haloed with light,
as if cast there by the Big-Bang.)

What on earth are you doing, I said,
you look ridiculous.

Some boys buried me here,
she said sullenly.

Her dark hair, comet-like, trailed behind...

Squatting, I pulled the
turnip up by the root.

*[In the aftermath of the bombing, many survivors moved into the foothills of the
Chugoku mountains surrounding Hiroshima. This was the case with Yasusada and his
daughter.]

AWKWARD FRAGMENT AND BOYFRIEND
December 29, 1945

These are, she said, her arms held out,
my only arms, and I must be
done with it before they
come. And then the flowers blossomed
upon her back. (And then)*
the transparent coat of dreams
enclosed her sex. (And then) she
was transported—sly torso of the sign,
awkward fragment— by the
Boyfriend of Compassionate Tears,

[Yasusada notes at bottom of page]
(fit in the phrase, "immaculate sphere descending")

(to clench in his virgin palm (...)—see Genji)

(Describe in a heading the dream of Akiko's voice.)

*[Parentheses in text are Yasusada's. While the term "Fragment" appears intended to
figuratively suggest an archeological image, it seems, as well, to appropriately prefigure
the fragmented nature of this draft.]*

[The following letter is undated, but its contents reveal it was written sometime in the first winter subsequent to the bombing of Hiroshima. Written to Akutagawa Fusei, (who, along with Ozaki Kusatao was Yasusada's closest friend and literary associate), it may be read as a letter of condolence regarding Fusei's young son, Masahito, who died of radiation sickness a few months after the bombing. The letter, handwritten in ink on stationary, is heavily blotched by dampness, and its middle section is largely illegible. We have translated the identifiable—and fortuitously beautiful—fragments of this section and placed them here in their approximate location in the original text. Whether this is an original letter that was never sent or a draft that was copied over and mailed before or after its source was damaged, we do not know. The fragmented middle section (although we cannot be entirely certain here) seems to refer to the great rise in Hiroshima, following the city's destruction, of evangelical forms of Pure Land Buddhism that placed special emphasis on the veneration of the buddha Amida. Both Yasusada and Fusei were serious lay practitioners of Zen, and the fragments seem to hint at a criticism of the belief in "otherworldly" salvation that is promised by Amidism.

Nomura, Yasusada's wife, perished in the bombing. Akiko is his adolescent daughter, who suffered from radiation sickness before her death in 1949.]

Dear Fusei:

Night before last was the first falling of snow on Hiroshima since the bombing. A full moon, and I walked alone for one or two miles before dawn, a quilt sewn by Nomura about me, Akiko's old school socks pulled up my arms. *How cleansed the ruins seemed of any guilt or repentance, of any pity or remorse. There was a clarity and peace into which I dissolved. There was an emptiness populated by forms that happened to be. * I* thought of you then, my friend, and yearned with all my heart *[illegible due to blotching].* And yet later, holding her *[Akiko, eds.]* as she wept and muttered in her half-sleep, the grief welled up in me again, and swallowed the whole world.

Most all Hiroshima
          Lotus Sutra   Amida Butsu   relief
But   Heart Sutra   most need   open to
          flat directness

                              emptiness, emptiness   form

          pure land not beyond   here

but form.   no Amida   Hiroshima your pain, simply

                              pain

        drinking and gazing at the sky on the night Masahito was
born, the stars were both real and not real, their light finding us in our
own time out of an extinguished time. Your joy *[illegible due to blotching]*
But surely the pleasure and wonder we felt then is still fully here in you
and in me. Here, amidst the night-sky's light that touches this snow and
traces the half-walls of this home and that. My home and your home.
[extended illegible passage due to blotching] then children will cry out in
joy, or curl in sorrow like autumn leaves. It is not for us *[illegible due to
blotching]* to be done about it. Such rising and falling is endless and
without explaining. I live and you live in that, and in that doubled flow-
ering the departed and the living are blessed as one.

Please write to me when you can,

[The italics are ours. Yasusada is quoting here, curiously, from the opening page of
The Tear Soaked Pillow, *an anonymous and pornographic diary dating from the
Heian era.]*

LOON AND DOME
January 1, 1947

The crying girl sounds like a loon . . .

Why does her mournful sound call to mind the sky
through the dome of the Industrial Promotion Hall?[1]

You told me there you were pregnant with her
as we strolled through the plaster chambers
of the giant Model of the Heart.

I have waited all week, you quietly said,
to be with you here in this magical place,
and to tell you something beautiful.

(It was your sentimental heart
that always made me laugh,
and this stain on the page is spilt tea.)[2]

[Yasusada note in margin] Insert breast-plate stanza here?

Nomura, the long wake of our daughter
vanishes, ceaselessly, in our union.

*[1. The Hiroshima Industrial Promotion Hall, a prominent city landmark because of its
windowed dome, was one of the few structures left somewhat recognizable after the
bombing. Its skeletal remains have been preserved to the present as a memorial.
2. In the original, there is, indeed, a stain covering the first half of the poem.]*

GEISHA AND IRIS *
May 4, 1947

(Bought the liver with rusty coins.)

(Walked in a hill's direction.)

(Chanced to find an iris.)

(Unnaturally large for sure.)

(Plucked it with a sexual longing.)

(This was at the edge of the radius-sweep.)

(Though flowers beyond are also large.)

(Two prefectures from here.)

(As the stick and mud home was as I'd left it.)

(Random chickens most happy.)

(A small garden doing well.)

(Gazed at the photo of the sultry geisha.)

(On newspaper liver was wrapped in.)

(While eating liver with radish.)

(Beneath the iris which was towering.)

[Parentheses in text are Yasusada's.]

July 14, 1948

The fascist is young—
Why does he carry a teapot
among the graves?

[undated]

having called her
a few names
I notice the age
in my hand

August 5, 1947

Summer dream—
a wandering moth fans its wings
on Akiko's brow

TROLLEY FARE AND BLOSSOM
—for my daughter, Akiko, 1930-1949
May 18, 1949

How can I tell you now
that the fire's warmth was pleasurable
on my body?[1]

Your body enveloped by it
and somehow, still, by mine.

The round urn, so finely cut,
each blade of grass bent black
against a black moon. You, weightless
within it.

How embarrassing, I thought, cupping it before me,
if in the middle of this ceremony I
stumbled, kabuki-like, and fell!

Thus, bearing you, and weeping,
I paid the trolley fare.

How to tell you now
of this simple happiness,
of the children laughing in a ring
at Hiroshima's heart, the brushstrokes
falling fast and light?[2]

You, Akiko, thick branch
on which this scentless blossom
is breaking.[3]

[1. This refers, at least literally, to his daughter's cremation.
2. The poem, guarded in a rice paper sheath, is in ink calligraphy. See Frontispiece.
3. A somewhat amateurish sumi drawing (we believe by Yasusada himself) of a flowering branch, runs down the right side of the page.]

RICE AND BONES WAKA
May 20, 1949*

Tugging her spilled rice

from the black-bear rug

I have become the bones

of this young pine's shade

[Five days after Akiko's death.]

TRILOBYTES
December 15, 1949
  —I dedicate this poem to the potter, Sakutaro Ishihara (1897-1949)

Only last month I was drunk with him
in Koi, at the Soto Bar. He had come
from his treatment and seemed overly excited.

Suddenly from his burlap-bag he raised
a concave stone and placed it, gently,
in the space between us.

And what have we here?, I said, with a great curiosity.

The fossils of trilobytes!, he whispered, leaning
forward, as if sharing a sexual secret.

(The waiter appeared over us, clutching a vase
of sake, his long geisha-nails like contrails
against the black lacquer. . .)

Where on earth did you come upon this?, I inquired.

Why at the Central Museum. . .
A fossil collection donated by the Americans. . .
A challenge to get past the guards!

We both laughed deeply then, and for a moment
I could see, beneath the scarred flesh,
the beautiful face of his youth. . .

I gazed at him, gazing at the fossil:
The clumps of hair on his skull, the hands
curled into claws. Was he thinking
of his pottery, all of it, scattered into atoms?

This morning I cradled the stone
through the ruins, past the shadows of bodies,
and bowing to his memory
placed it,
soundlessly,
at the epicenter.

ECHO AND VISITORS
[undated]

(The program-brochure revealing in English that,
"according to tradition, the thud-slap of bodies is an
echo which reaches us, lapping, from the Pure Land")[1]

Lovely,
the wrestler's head,
oil-glazed, hair pulled back
to the intricate knot.

He crouches, shameless,
in the ring and is still,
drawing the breath, I think,
of the pleasure-seekers
into him.

Soundless,
flesh forgotten, he coils
to absorb the fullness
of the
Pure Land...

(And you, Nomura,
in your morning kimono,
the name of our daughter
half-called as she strolls
the thistle-lined path...) [2]

The force of the meeting astounds the visitors.

*[1. In looseleaf, the poem appears to have been written during the occupation. The
"English" program Yasusada mentions would be explained by the great popularity
Sumo wrestling enjoyed among American soldiers.*
*2. The lineation in the third and fourth stanzas is our approximation, as Yasusada's
arrows and brackets indicating rearrangement are unclear.]*

[undated]

[Yasusada note] (For "last moments" poem. To be written in katakana characters.)

the tabi-sneakers arranged neatly by the door
(the three pairs).

the pickling tubs throwing their long morning shadows
(but don't risk moralizing).

the small daughter brushing-off her school uniform
(the static-sound).

a history of Japan in twelve volumes
(the dust-film).

palms, because of unseasonly heat put out their buds
(is such a thing possible?).

the Father, running late, scowling and sponging the bear-skin rug
(elaborate the oddity).

a gargoyle, broken-off, lying near the wall
(is this believable?).

the child, his loud suckling at the Mother's breast
(their locked eyes).

[Jotted by Yasusada at bottom of page] Ujina Bay—oysters, cultural center, book store district, Hiji Hill, Kokutaji temple, Asano library

January 5, 1953

Dear Kurihara Tadaichi:

I wish to thank you for the kind invitation to contribute to the planned anthology *Poetry Hiroshima*.* It was very thoughtful of Tokuno Koichi to suggest my name, but I must convey to you that his estimation of my abilities far exceeds the actual case. You see, what little scribbling I occasionally do hardly deserves to be called "poetry," and I fear that should any of it appear in public, that it would cause me more embarrassment than satisfaction, and the reader more confusion than edification!

Nevertheless, I wish you the greatest fortune in this project, and also extended success with your magazine *Chugoku Culture*. And I will look forward, certainly, to seeing the book. Reading, at least, is one thing I do well.

With my most respectful wishes,

---

*[In carbon. Poetry Hiroshima *was published in 1954. The largest of all "atomic bomb" literature anthologies, it contained over 1700 poems by 220 poets. Yasusada's false modesty and reluctance to contribute is revealing indeed, and supports our conviction that his anonymity was purposely cultivated.* Chugoku Culture *was one of the two major literary journals of post-war Hiroshima. We are ignorant of Tokuno Koichi's identity.]*

CHRYSANTHEMUMS AND SHOES *
August 9, 1953

Thus drunk, I pulled off my shoes.

Inside they were dark, cave-like,
with a distant bat-like smell.

Are there wing-sounds in the dark?

I placed my shoes over my large ears...

No... no bats in there...

Thoughtful, I recalled the girl
from the Eastern outskirts
whom I had deeply desired.

The night that was our first meeting
I put on a suit and polished my shoes
to a glare.

Nervously, I knocked on her door,
hiding chrysanthemums behind my back.

Good Morning!, I cried.

You mean Good Evening, she said,
smiling softly.

Oh, yes, of course, I said,
looking down at my shoes, I
mean Good Evening.

Later, sipping sake on a mat,
I admired her long, pearl-colored feet...

You have such beautiful feet, I declared,
I hope you don't mind me saying so!

And you, she murmured with downcast
eyes, are quite the charmer, aren't you?

Walking home that evening I felt
so happy and light, sure that I
had made the finest impression.

The quiet of sleep had fallen
over Hiroshima, and moonlight tipped
the buildings and pines...

Sighing, I lowered the shoes from my
ears, and placed them beneath my bed,
like two small boats,
side by side.

[It would appear likely that this poem refers to the courtship of Yasusada and Nomura.]

[undated]

two daikons

three rice cakes

one [blotted by crease, eds.] seaweed packet

4 crane eggs

empress oil   chrysanthemum root   best rice

*Bear yourself with a serious air through the labyrinth of the
market. Feign to ignore the [blotted by crease, eds.] spirit medium of
plum-colored lips*

American cologne

*[Despite the curious interjection, this appears to be a shopping list. It was found in one
of the notebooks, folded into an origami bird.]*

September 20, 1953

Dear Fusei:

Chuya Kaneko was here *[in Hiroshima, eds.]* for an exhibit of his work at Shiraga's place.[1] Indescribably wonderful. The photographs I sent you last year communicate little of the power, but our instincts as to his essential impulse were correct: It is fundamentally at one with our faith in the great depth that tradition holds out. He and a group of co-workers have recently formed a group tethered to Genbi *[short for Contemporary Art Committee]* called Men of Ink, with a periodical called *The Beauty of Ink*. There was a party at Tomio's home after the exhibit (all the works were bought!), and I ended up, delightfully, speaking with Chuya for about forty-five minutes, sharing with him three of our renga: "Prefectural Bamboo," "Food and Sake Pleasures," and "Momoyama Hat Dance." To my great pleasure (and I'm sure yours) he invited us to attend a group meeting, so as to have us read a few of our pieces. He proposed, in fact, an interest in painting a series of pieces based on a renga of ours—one small canvass for each line; I then proposed that the three of us would in turn compose a new renga based on his calligraphic interpretations of the first.[2] His response was thus: He lit a Lucky Strike cigarette, blew a sequence of impeccable smoke rings, and said, "It is only inside the alphabet that there are mountains and rivers, don't you think?" A magnificent man.

So I think it is essential that Fusei *[Yasusada means Kusatao]* and I try to meet with you in Nishinomiya sometime soon. The Men of Ink are very interested, like us, in the hidden interfacements between East and West; I'm sure much would come of our association with these artists, who at bottom are working with our medium *[i.e. language]*.

Are you as excited by the promise of it as I? We realize you are more constrained with time, but it is only twenty or so kilometers away, is it not?[3] Kusatao and I look forward to hearing from you on the dates you would have available. The group meets on the second and fourth Saturday of each month. Please write soon.[4]

I've been working on a few new Dickinson translations, which I will send to you soon.[5] It is slow, difficult work; there are layers and layers there... Kusatao is mostly through the hepatitis, and sends his warm regards to you and the family.

My heartiest greetings,

[1. In carbon. Chuya Kaneko (1920-1991) was a member of the Bokujin Kai (The Men of Ink), a group of Japanese artists that was active in the 1950's. Led by Morita Shiryu (1915-) The Men of Ink were interested in the abstract possibilities of calligraphy and, in particular, in the affinities between experimental calligraphic art and American Abstract Expressionism. The more encompassing Contemporary Art Committee (or Genbi) was led by Yoshihara Jiro (1901-1972); it later evolved into the Concrete Art Association (or Gutai), which was very closely allied with the international avant-garde movements during the late 50's and 60's. The identity of Shiraga and Tomio is unknown to us.

2. Three "calligraphy" samples were found, carefully guarded with rice paper covering, in a separate portfolio found among Yasusada's belongings. Though unsigned, it is our belief (and that of experts we have consulted with) that the pieces are by Chuya, and are perhaps part of an intended series accompanying a renga by Yasusada, Fusei, and Kusatao.

3. Yasusada refers here to the distance between Nishinomiya and Osaka, both being in the province of Kansai. Chuya's group was based in Nishinomiya. Both Fusei and Kusatao worked for the Ohiro Insurance Company after the war, and were transferred back and forth periodically, between Hiroshima and Osaka.

4. No other references to the Men of Ink are present in the notebooks presently in our hands. The renga mentioned by Yasusada are not present either.

5. Apparently a reference to the great American poet, Emily Dickinson. No other reference to her, or drafts of Yasusada's translations from her work, are in our hands.]

HIGH ALTITUDE PHOTO OF HIROSHIMA (CIRCA 1944)
March 7, 1957

—I dedicate this poem to the great artist, Piet Mondrian*

There must be a schoolgirl deep inside there, stuttering,
almost weeping, to remember the main cities
of our ally, Germany.

There must be a monk, self-absorbed, slowly dragging
his rake through sand, around a moss-covered stone.

A man inside his home has thrown a little boy into the air:
The child is there, falling, his mouth open with joy.

And I. . . where am I? For being here is confusing,
makes my position less clear. Somewhere in the upper left,
I suppose, hurrying ambitiously to get somewhere . . .

I shut my eyes, try to recall those days . . .

Outside of me the photograph is beautiful and clear:
A long, single pulse of geometry under dreams.
Pure hieroglyph into which I also will vanish.

* [The work of Mondrian, Dutch artist and major figure of the modernist avant-garde,
is distinguished by its geometric austerity.]

WALKERS WITH LADLE
[undated]

—I dedicate this poem to Javier Alvarez (1906-1945)[1]

They walk in the echo. They walk darkly, like mediums. They walk out of step, they walk with *[illegible, eds.]*[2] and supplications beyond the audible. They walk on their buttocks with the *[illegible]* but they walk with a bottomless conviction.

You are not to forget it: They walk pushing their being out from within, they walk as if they were carried forth by another, they walk in terror, confident and full, hollowed out by the ladle, and with the fervor of the converted.

And they walk like no one walks. They keep walking, and then when lying down by the side of another they keep walking. They walk awake and asleep, they walk backwards with enormous genitals, they walk in circles with rose-wood chopsticks, they walk face-down, moaning in the mud for *[illegible]* They walk out of step, walking in the sentimental garlands of *[illegible]* blatherings.

And they walk as if someone had commanded: *Don't you dare fucking walk you fucking Jap fucker.*[3]

Thus with the clock frozen at the given hour, they know and don't know where they walk. But it carries them to the river's stagnant smile *[illegible]* and they walk out of step.

Our wounds close up before we pass Him again.

[Yasusada note at bottom of page] Kusatao was over today and said this sounds like a bad translation from Italian or Spanish poetry.[4] So I'm onto something! (But what is that something, in the end? That is the question.)

[1. Javier Alvarez was a poet and Bolivian consul to Hiroshima during the war years. We gather he was an acquaintance of Yasusada and, from the death-date, that he perished in the bombing.
2. The numerous illegible sections are due to erasures in the original penciled text.
3. In English in original.
4. Indeed, passages here seem to be very liberal "translations" from Dante's Inferno.*]*

BLOSSOMS AND SCREAM
May 5, 1959

They must love the Earth in a simple way:
boy's Karate Club, lined on the young grass,
hands clenched with such intensity.

They must love the open parentheses of the blossoms,
still in their sheaths: Basho Chapter in a circle
of chairs, pencils poised.

I love the hard words the adolescents say:
weird, cool, far-out, banzai . . .
And the softer words of the old:
*oh my, deary, the ways of heaven . . .**

I feel a strange happiness on this day,
May 5, 1959, Peace Memorial Park.

The green and yellow belts let out
a scream, shoot forward a hundred fists.

A man puts his pencil down, looks up
at the blossoms and smiles.

I look over his shoulder and read:

[Yasusada note] Insert haiku April 11, 1959

*[Italicized phrases are cultural approximations for the Japanese idioms contained in the
original. Given Yasusada's concluding note—which seems to intend the inclusion of
one of his own haiku—it appears possible that the poem may be a fictional construction.
No haiku with the indicated date has been found in the notebooks.]*

TELESCOPE WITH URN
February 14, 1960

The image of the galaxies spreads-out like a cloud of sperm.

Expanding, said the observatory guide, and at such and such velocity.

It is like the idea of the flowers, opening within the idea of the
flowers.

I like to think of that, said the monk, arranging them with his
papery fingers.

Tiny were you, and squatted over a sky-colored bowl to make water.

What a big girl! cried we, tossing you in the general direction of
the stars.

Intently, then, in the dream, I folded up the great telescope on
Mount Horai.

In the form of this crane, it is small enough for the urn.

[Yasusada was a lay zennist during most of his adult life and apparently attended sesshin (two to three day meditation sessions) on a regular basis. The following group, apparently recordings of dokusan encounters (brief Zen teacher/student interviews, where the student may challenge the teacher), was found in a World War II military postal service envelope inserted into one of the notebooks. Each undated piece is written on separate sheets or scraps of paper.]

"who is the one before me?" I said.

"two sticks and one clack," he said.

"oh," I said, "so this one is three?"

"no," he said, "but you, unfortunately, would still appear to be."

"so what is the difference between noumena and phenomena?" I said.

"one," he said.

"one?" I said.

"you said it," he said.

His ten fingernails were golden in the sun.

A mosquito fed, plumply, on his brow.

"become this one," he said.

"Isn't what *mu* is 'about,'" I said, "exactly its own aboutness?" *

"This 'aboutness,'" he said, fanning himself with the *Morning News*, "Why do you think it, or anything, has a "ness"?

*[*Apparently an attempted response by Yasusada to a first koan traditionally given to Zen students. In many cases, years pass before the student satisfactorily "solves" it: "What is the meaning of mu?" In tiny characters, going around the edges of the paper, which is torn from a standard notebook sheet, Yasusada has penned, "This would have been a good question to ask Herr Heidegger?" The added note, compared to the faded quality of the ink recording the dokusan, appears fresh, leading us to assume that it was added at a considerably later date, most probably after 1964, when Heidegger's* Being and Time *was first published in Japanese translation.]*

My teacher said, "Thoughts are empty."

I said, " But isn't that a thought, that thoughts are empty?"

He lit a cigarette, inhaled deeply, and blew out the smoke in a faint, long line. I could see the pines through the window moving behind him. Sunlight moving here, there, on the mats.

"And so," he coughed, "Where is the ground of the thought in which you are standing now?"

My teacher said, "Yun-men Wen-yen said: 'The universe is so vast and wide, up, down, sideways, and so on. Why do you put on your priest's robe at the sound of the bell?'"

There was a long silence. A dog cried out from somewhere, yelped off in pain. The moon shone on the gaudy geisha fan, splayed in sequins across his lap. The air-raid drill siren in Hiroshima rose and fell, faintly, beyond the hills.

"Well, I don't always," I said. "I seem to be tiring in my practice, and have had trouble, this *sesshin*, promptly answering the morning bell."

"Well," he said, "I was only telling you what Yun-men Wen-Yen *said*. Personal difficulties, in this case, are quite beside the point."

My teacher said, "strive to become entangled, completely, in the dharma."

Here now, on the pyre, his body erupts into flames.

[undated]

—for Ishikawa Aishin Zenji (1874–1960)

Through the bluish snow
the abbot has gone
into the joyous young pines

April 2, 1960

Holding an X-ray
I allow hundreds of geese
to enter my life

December 12, 1960

Silent screen—
so many lives flickering
in both rooms

[Yasusada note at bottom of page] "Silent screen": a painted dividing
screen from, say, the Edo, or the fluttering image of, say, Buster Keaton.
Or the two fused into one, and so on.

CONVALESCENCE *
August 20, 1961

Today, strolling alone,
outside the convalescent hospital, I
paused and tucked in my chin: Why,
this fresh scar dividing my chest
is like the opening stroke
of calligraphy
on an empty scroll!

In these flat Shinoda fields, under the flat
sky, day is a glazed tile of intricate
detail. Neither I, nor the lotus,
nor the tiny sparrows pacing delicately
on the tatami mats, will ever take leave of it . . .

Out of breath I entered the bubbling pool
and knitted my brow: Since when we gaze at the stars
we gaze into a vanished past, is not night, Nomura,
the rough underside of the tile?

I waited for her answer, feeling
my pulse, drying outstretched
on a bed of moss. . .

As I returned along the slate path,
cranes, faintly shimmering in dusk,
fished in the fields of rice.

Crackling underfoot were the shells
of cicadas who had gone,
screaming like samurai,
more deeply into the pattern.

*[The poem seems to indicate that Yasusada underwent open heart surgery a short time
before the date of this poem.]*

March 15, 1962

Dear Fusei:[1]

I am sending you here a poem I have fashioned, made out of various pieces of teachings by Kusho Roshi, here at Joei Temple, imparted to me personally, as well as to the sangha *[community of monks and lay practitioners, eds.]* as a whole in lecture. The remarks are from my memory, and if not perfectly accurate, they are at least free from conscious embellishment. I give this poem a special place, for I feel it does manage to fuse its form, in a pure and undirected way, with the occasion of its becoming.

What I imagine you have heard from Kyojin by now is true: I dozed-off during kinhin *[walking-meditation]* at sesshin *[very extended meditation session]* and bumped into the magnificent Edo chamber-pot at the North end of the hall. It had been sitting there for some two hundred years (Ikkyu[2] himself is said to have done his necessities in it!), and I watched it slowly tip and fall to crash against the floor. Pointless to attempt to describe my feelings of despair at that moment, and those feelings I harbored until the following day when I met with Roshi in dokusan *[traditional teacher-student interview]* and stuttered the apology that serves as the poem's title. The Roshi's gentle answer makes up the last line of the poem.

It is amazing, but, you know, when the vase shattered and all the monks startled-up and turned in their tracks, Roshi at once snapped his whisk to the floor and bellowed out: *Where monks? Where is the cause of your distraction?* It was then that the sun broke through day-long clouds, and suffused the hall with a golden glow. The coincidence enters the practice . . .

And how is your own study coming along? And the family is as well as can be, I hope? I must rush-off now, but please write to me soon.

Affectionately,

[1. In carbon, the letter is attached to the following poem in one of the notebooks.
2. Ikkyu Sojun (1394-1481), poet, painter, and great eccentric Zen master of the Rinzai school.]

41

"I am sorry to have broken the ancient chamber pot. I feel terribly about it."

"That the path of leaving is the path of becoming."

"It is the song the smallest thing is always singing."

"So study the track of the wave-washed shell."

"Thus delighting in the distances of things."

"After all, the sutra does not say that words and reality are one."

"But thank you for the beautiful book that you gave me."

"So before coming in, please take off your shoes."

"So before eating, be sure to boil the flowers."

"After all, there is no question there are worlds beyond this one."

"Of course, it is thoughtful to say so, but the furniture is
not there to be 'admired.'"

"Yes, it is pleasant to think so."

"Nor, in the end, does the sutra deny it."

"What is it you want from your life?"

"There are plenty more pots where that one came from."

[undated]

American circus—
the Japanese midget wears the body
of a horse

[undated]

amidst condoms washed up on the beach
a plastic dinosaur bears its teeth

[undated]

Wetly adorning
the monk's behind—
veined side
of the golden leaf

SARCOPHAGUS AND MARACAS
August 10, 1962
-Summer sesshin, Joei Temple, service for Koetsu-

Fat, he was the butt of jokes,
farting his sake smell in zazen, chanting for alms
in sleep. Now his bed's rolled-up,
like a rare shell, begging bowl inside.

The sarcophagus is slanted upward,
as if travelling at great speed.
"Plenty of solid fuel for this zen-rocket!",
he'd blurt-out while chiseling, making us howl.
How could he keep forgetting, we marvelled,
that he'd said it before?

Filing by, we now read his last waka, set
deeply in the granite hood:

Why waver over meanings?
Moon silvering all,
absorb the tracks of birds
on this spit of sand.

Sotatsu's egrets, brittle, hung for the occasion,
soar in emptiness above . . .

So in this newspaper photo they too
seem to want to make us laugh:
Four mariachis at Peace Park,
open-mouthed and looking skyward,
shaking their maracas . . .

[Yasusada was a lay Zennist and became a resident student for a brief period during the early 1960's. The heading date and last stanza are entered in a different colored ink than the rest of the poem. "Maracas" has also been appended to the title—inscribed above the crossed-out characters for "Tracks." The poem's title and waka of the fourth stanza are in Japanese; the rest of the poem is in English. Peace Park is built on the flash-point site of the atomic bomb. Sotatsu was a Zen priest and painter of the late 16th-early 17th centuries. See Javier del Azar's letter and score on pages 103-108 for more related to this poem.]

[undated]

riding the pick-up
monks of various ages
have vanished into distance

DREAM AND CHARCOAL
[undated]

And then she said: I have gone toward the light and become beautiful.

And then she said: I have taken a couple of wings and attached them to the various back-parts on my body.

And then she said: all the guests are coming back to where they were and then talking.

To which she said: without the grasp-handle, how would you recognize my nakedness?

To which she replied: without nothing is when all things die.

Which is when she had a wild battle with the twigs.

Which is when the charcoal was passed from her body to mine.

Which was how she rose into the heavens, blinding the pedestrians.

Which was how our union was transposed into a dark scribble.

Which became the daughter calling, calling my name to wake me.

January 4, 1964

Penis withered
I follow a begging bowl
into hailstones

August 12, 1964

The sake-shop hisses with its pleasures, all boiled up.

Here the young are speaking of virility and all the hidden forms.

Language on the window is backwards here, and inside
the glass the small cries or clicks of things might be taken as the
spirits of the flowers, in the Garden of the Ungathered . . .

There is the blur of the child, dropping from the tree.

Here is a black-haired man with a black-haired man.

There are the two sticks and a cup in Spring.

Here is a sake-burned mouth and the account of the lost cranes.

*Here is a young bride's half-turned face, which is turning, as it
must, to be turned towards me.**

*[The italicized text—with the exception of the cryptic line "Here is a sake-burned
mouth. . . ."—is clearly a reference to an outdoor photograph of Nomura, found among
the pages of one of the notebooks. As with much else in the notebooks, it is unclear
whether Yasusada considered this as finished, or as a draft for further elaboration. The
lines in italics are written in katakana characters in original.]*

UTTERANCES AND HEPATICA
[undated]

And then he said, there is a language and I make it.

And then he replied, don't take the ancient engravings so solemnly.

And then he said, I want to crawl away and hide in the thought to which I am leading.

To which she inquired, why are you so certain about the utterances of the Tokyo people?

And then she read, "Kikuyu is a very sad case. She made a bad marriage, and she came here afterwards."

And then she screamed, if a man had a tough hairy hide, his world would be different indeed.

Which is when he threw her bath utensils randomly to the tile.

Which is when he imagined her body as the portal of a valley.

Which is when she touched herself in sorrow amidst hepatica.

Which shall be the queen of all flowers.

So this was written in the egg-laying season of the moths.

So in such a time their body is swollen beyond all proportion to their wings.

Which was when someone lifted her solemnly toward the clouds.

Which was when the radius of the area was reproduced a large number of times.

Which was on a day the suitor was bearing a large bouquet of hepatica.

Which shall be the queen of all flowers.

March 30, 1935

Dear Ogiwara Seisensui:

Would you kindly share this modest gathering of haiku at the April
meeting? I would appreciate your communicating to Taneda [Santoka]
and [Ozaki] Hosai that their criticisms from last month were seriously
pondered. My hope is that an echo of their insight might be present
here. Please give everyone my warmest greetings. I am feeling better,
and I do believe it will be possible to travel next month. Will Santoka
and Ozaki be at the May meeting?

I stretch out my hands to you— We share a single sky,

Yasusada*

iris   moon   sheaths

scubadivers   chrysanthemums   also

deer   inlets   dream

oars   this   earth

geese   lined   bowl

shard   so   horizon

cod   dried   dawn

bones   sky   written

lichened   space   rock

fossils   celebrating   investors

crematorium   shared   persimmon

hyacinth   clustered   strangers

cranes   three   words

*[In carbon, with Yasusada's signature. We do not know what illness Yasusada refers to as having inhibited his travel, though it was perhaps of some seriousness, given Yasusada's young age at the time. Ogiwara Seisensui (1884-1976), one of the great figures of modern Japanese haiku, was founder and coordinator of the Soun (Layered Clouds) haiku group in which Yasusada was active from the early 1930's. The Soun poets, extending earlier gestures of Kawahigashi Hekigodo (1873-1937), revolutionized the practice of haiku by breaking decisively with traditional constraints, most notably syllable count. Santoka (1882-1940) and Hosai (1885-1926) are perhaps its most famous figures. Yasusada and Seisensui were to have a falling-out in the late 1950's, largely over a prolonged debate within the group on matters pertaining to renga composition. The letter of Yasusada to Seisensui that follows suggests some of the issues that gave rise to later tensions.]

JUNE 2, 1937

Dear Ogiwara Seisensui:

Kusatao and Fusei have reported back to me on the May meeting. I am writing to convey my profound disappointment at the reaction to the three new renga we presented there. Disappointing, too, that once again the Hiroshima poets have found themselves last on the agenda, when attention tends, inevitably, to wane. Allow me to say that if I have received a fair account of the proceedings, the tone of the criticisms would seem to have been rather patronizing and contrary to the spirit that has always guided the *Soun*. As I have understood it, that spirit has been one of exploring our poetic traditions with unfettered freedom and infusing them with the spirit of actual life.

In what way is what we have presented "beyond the province of litera-ture," as Shuoshi, I am told, remarked while others seriously nodded? Mind you, I am most willing to concede Shuoshi's point, as this category, and the pretentious assumptions that buttress it, interest me little . . . But why is it less worthy of being considered in the realm of the "literary" than the free-form haiku all of us have been writing? Is Shuoshi's charge not really an echo of that leveled against *Strata*[1] for the past fifteen years by Kyoshi?[2] Clearly, a more rigorous discussion is needed; clearly, as well, there needs to be a healthy (and calm) exchange about the renga, begin-ning with the theory of Yoshimoto and Basho. I invoke the masters, because the hostility of the group is misdirected from the standpoint of the oldest renga traditions themselves! Thus if the linking seems impure, as it has been criticized to be, it is precisely because we have embraced the reality and promise of impurity; if the stanzas seem shorn of poetic con-vention, it is precisely because we aim to transcend the assumptions of "poetry", so as to see what might lay beyond. Indeed, our heroes are the "no-thought poets" of the late Edo, who held the sweetness of dissonance to be the deep measure of renga. Their path of pulling mind into the mar-row of language itself is our path. For in the suchness of utterance there is as much mystery as in all the plum blossoms of the *Manyoshu* (though you know that I still love the *Manyoshu*).

Of course this will all seem rushed. And I trust you understand that my impatience is not with you. I have heard that you were silent through-out the exchange at the meeting. Still, we are eager to know your views about this difference. To our minds, in these times when renga is going the way of the tea-ceremony, nothing less than its lifeblood is at stake.

Your student,

[1. *Journal of the Soun. We are unsure of the identity of Shuoshi.*
2. *Takahama Kyoshi. See letter of May 30, 1957, p. 53-54*]

*[undated]**

Talking about the weather
a stick runs through our mouths
the blossoms are fragrant

[The poem is written on the back of a fire-singed photograph of Yasusada and the great itinerant haiku poet, Taneda Santoka. They are in profile, speaking. A flowering branch traverses the picture, and gives, indeed, the appearance of mutually penetrating the open mouths of the figures. Given the date of Santoka's death from the effects of alcoholism, the photograph is from 1940 or earlier. This is (or was) one of the very few remaining images, anywhere, of Santoka. The photograph was contained in a notebook that was tragically lost in transit from Japan.]

[undated]

[Yasusada note in margin] Send to Santoka

Slate bed—I dream of genitals at an angle

*

Cool night—the rag tipped with moon

*

Chrysanthemum's scent—no hail under the long rock

*

Obediently bowing—the white flowers

*

Sake's transparent—I pat the pig

*

The wild grasses—so here I am

*

I dream of my daughter—the silk-worm farm

[The following letter was found in carbon. Takahama Kyoshi (1874-1959) was, with Kawahigashi Hekigoto, the great haiku master Masaoka Shiki's (see "Because I Live" p. 118-119 most important student. In 1898 Kyoshi founded Hototogisu, *(The Cuckoo), which was for many decades Japan's most important journal of haiku and related literature. As main editor, Kyoshi steadfastly used* Hototogisu *as a forum for traditionalist literary values. The* Soun, *(Layered Clouds), led by Ogiwara Seisensui–who took up Hekigoto's rebelliousness–was the most influential experimental haiku group in mid-century Japan and the Hototogisu group's main contricant (see other entries in text for further discussion of Layered Clouds). A review of 1957 and early 1958 issues of* Hototogisu *reveals that the letter was never published. This is not surprising, perhaps, given the subtle but cutting sarcasm in Yasusada's remarks.]*

May 30, 1957

Esteemed Gentlemen:

Mr. Takahama Kyoshi, in his monthly column in *Hototogisu,* May 2, refers to the poets of the Layered Clouds as "merely paddling their small boats up the tributaries of language" and compares the verse of his own school, "written in the speech of common life," with the "wide and steady flowing of the Mogami River." Mr. Kyoshi's poetry is dearly loved by great numbers of people in our land, and his deep talent is beyond dispute. But I would like, in the spirit of fraternal exchange, to offer a few questions and comments on Mr. Kyoshi's figurative comparison.

Why are tributaries less viable or interesting (as Mr. Kyoshi clearly implies) than the wide, broad river? After all, tributaries tend— although narrower in width [*sic*] and more modest in volume—to be less eroded and silted, more topographically accidented, and generally more welcoming of diverse plant and animal life. There is more lush vegetation there, more coves and hidden inlets (the pirates of the Heian always hid their treasures in these spots, away from the commerced lanes of our waterways, and archeologists are still uncovering them!). Mr. Kyoshi must know, too, as a devotee of fly-fishing,[1] that at certain times of the year, the biggest salmon and sea-run trout are found in the smallest streams. One would certainly deny oneself the full pleasures of angling by fishing the largest river on every occasion.

Above all, a fundamental natural truth should be noted: The main river cannot survive in a healthy, biologically rich way in the absence of tributaries. Tributaries are not incidental, secondary, or parasitical, but essential to the very *existence* of the broad river; they cleanse the river of impurities, and they infuse it with new life.

Of course, one cannot argue with the importance of keeping the main currents open and unobstructed. Barges of trade and pleasure craft, waterskiers, picnickers, and so on, have their rights to passage. But certainly the tributaries might be regarded by mainstream writers with a bit less defensiveness[2] and a greater degree of ecological generosity.

Who knows? A cure for cancer or other stubborn diseases may yet be found in some unexplored backwater.

Sincerely,

[1. *Indeed, Kyoshi was an avid fly-fisher and occasional contributor to the monthly angling publication,* Nippon Salmonid.
2. *A word play in original: The Japanese term translated here as "defensiveness" is a verbal form of "impoundment".*]

October 25, 1963

Autumn Grasses Renga*

You see, he says courting her, the universe stretches forever without reason, or else stops somewhere without reason.

Beyond the flowering hedge are rows and rows of taro and radish.

Bending the spray of plum to her nose, she remembers her parents with a forced detachment.

At harvest, the unconscious motions of the workers are repeated again and again.

They have paused before the fallen nest woven of rice shoots.

She presses her ear to the wall, hearing the cries of the bride, as if they were not her own.

While pushing the perambulator through the darkened temple grounds, a trace of light remains near the top of the trees.

"The shortest way to the outhouse," hisses the monk, "is through that long patch of graves."

And so from the tea-kettle of birds comes the sound of wind-swept pines.

Nor will he ever forget the grove of lean saplings beneath the autumn moon.

"Whenever his left eye wanders outward," she confesses, "it causes me an uncontrollable irritation."

Wherefrom they argue over money near the dry and crumbled silk-worms.

"One could say romantic things, he says, but I resolutely refuse to do so."

Thus they part, taking different paths through stalks of dried sunflowers.

Now, to the sound of spring rain, he records his findings on a certain kind of mollusk.

He wants to write to them, but is afflicted with indecision.

Of course, he knows his daughter's acne is causing her much shame.

Some people are found still standing, burned to a dark crust.

In the photo, his wife's cosmetics and hair ornaments seem ordinary, recalling advertisements.

Slender autumn grasses are growing along the crest of an ancient earthen wall.

[By Yasusada, Ozaki Kusatao, and Akutagawa Fusei.]

FAKE TANKA
July 9, 1964

I smoke reading the *Manyoshu*
with crossed legs—
the dangling one
seems ancient now

April 24, 1965

Dear Kusatao:

I've composed these twenty one poems[1] by collaging lines and phrases from the *Kokinshu* and the *Manyoshu*.[2] Think of how many others there must be hidden within their pages!

I've been fairly well—a couple stays in hospital since we spoke last. The difficulty, as you know, is the sickness after treatment. Luckily the hospital wing they have me in looks out on the pine-covered hills of Mount Asano. I'll write again soon, but I must rush-off now. And you, you old fart—why don't you write *me?*

My affectionate regards to you and the family,

Yasusada

[1. *In carbon, with signature. The one here, numbered 19, is, unfortunately, the only one found in the notebooks. With the exception of most of the renga, the accompanying poem is one of the few that is typewritten.*
2. *The* Kokinshu *and* Manyoshu *are the two great classical collections of tanka poetry, from the Nara and Heian eras respectively. Despite Yasusada's assertion of working directly from these anthologies, we have been unable to locate any of the lines of his poem in either text, leading us to suspect that he is being playfully evasive with Kusatao.*]

19.

When I loved watching her take the wrong path
and calling her name to turn back.
A young maiden afraid to step on cicada shells and.
In a place of small flowers and the shadows of small flowers.
Where her voice would move toward the only window of.
Through which the sparrows flew in and out.
Through which the moon fell plainly upon the tatami mats.
And the dew of the blossoms was succulent to the prince.

November 17, 1965

Dear Kusatao:

I trust this hurried note finds you and the children in good health. As you might imagine, the news of your return to Hiroshima in September brings us much happiness. One can only hope the Company[1] will allow you to finally settle down now in one place! We will have much to discuss, and Fusei and I deeply look forward to renewing our collaboration.

Kuribayashi[2] returned from California last month and brought back books by six new American poets: Robert Duncan, Alex [sic] Ginsberg, John Wieners, Brother Antoninus, Philip Lamantia and Jack Spicer. They are all of the utmost interest, though we find ourselves most fascinated by Spicer. There are three collections of his work, printed with a delicacy that matches that of Dakotsu's *Isinglass*[3]: *Billy the Kid*, *The Heads of the Town Up to the Aether*, and *Language*. I believe our concerns are very similar to his, and I have just written him a letter, by way of one of the publishers, taking the liberty of sending him some of our renga.[4] I have begun to translate him, though this is proving to be very difficult indeed, and if I am to succeed, it will have to involve a correspondence with him. In any case, Fusei and I look forward to discussing the work of these most revealing poets with you.

I am sure you know of Seisensui's illness; the final break-up of Soun, I'm sure, has not helped him these past months. Perhaps the three of us can go to visit him in Tokyo after your return? It may well be our last chance to see the old radish-root.[5] Somehow the old battles have begun to seem so insignificant now... Did you know that I am working at the post office once again?

Write me with your plans so that we may greet you at the station.

My warm greetings,

[1. Ozaki Kusatao worked for the Ohiro Insurance Company and had been transferred to the Osaka Office.

2. Kuribayashi was an acquaintance of Yasusada, Fusei, and Kusatao. We have little other information about him. See letter of November 7, 1967, p. 76.

3. Iida Dakotsu (1885-1962) is one of the important haikuists of mid-century; close to Takahama Kyoshi's traditionalist wing, he edited Isinglass, one of the influential journals of the time.

4. In fact, Spicer had died only three months before the date of the above. No copy of Yasusada's correspondence to Spicer has been found. See also letter of November 7, 1967.

5. Seisensui actually went on to live for ten more years. It isn't clear whether the trip Yasusada refers to was ever made, though there is a partially missing 1966 sequence by the three entitled "Bullet Train Renga".]

April 2, 1966

LOVER'S RENGA*

There beneath the poplars and the comets we bent our heads toward each other.

"It is impossible to describe the beauty of the view. Words just can't even begin to express what I felt at that particular moment in time."

This is the geisha in the photograph, the one wearing skis.

Snow covered everything overnight. One of those sudden storms that come just when you think spring has arrived.

The curious notches in the mountain-face produced a meditative state in the search party.

At tea they mused in low voices about the disappearance of the old ways.

One acted laconic, while the other, a denizen, whirled her small bag of possessions like a weapon.

No, she confided, lowering her eyes, I did not come to see the flowers on Komako's grave.

Here is the faint trace of a line delimiting the relic.

Here is the offering of a sacred name which is [illegible, eds.].

Yet his icons seem strangely modern in their flatness and massing of forms, do they not?

Suddenly, while relic-viewing, she felt an erotic urge to relieve herself.

"I must tell you," he whispered into her deformed ear, "I don't think I have ever been happier in my entire wretched life."

Now lovers are parting, and the museum guide contemplates his heavy ring of keys.

The blossoms have broken early and with abandon.

An unusual amount of passerby are dressed in brilliantly patterned formal wear.

*[By Yasusada, Ozaki Kusatao, Akutagawa Fusei. A few of the lines in this renga are quotes or paraphrases from Kawabata Yasunari's The Snow Country.]

[undated]

I walk
flowing with something
and do not

[undated]

Temple bell—
inside the frozen raven
snow has fallen

September 2, 1966

NOVEAU RICHE RENGA*

—To the memory of Ishikawa Takuboku

Ants exult on the tense blossoms of the peonies.

So, calling names, the characters cluster or disperse in irregular designs.

(fifteen seconds, random, mokug yo)

"Isn't it a shame the farmers have almost forgotten the "Dance of the Clacking Sticks?" he asks.

"Squid in moonlight is bitter," she demurs, with affected indirection, gazing downward.

Manifold rays have converged to make this scene,' he thinks.

(extended noh-sigh)

A sign was written here long ago, and my whole life, in turn, she thinks.

(extended noh-sigh)

Now the moon has reached the zenith, which is also called the "Crotch of Paradise."

(fifteen seconds, random, mokug yo)

Now someone has forced a peony into his mouth, and dances drunken-ly before the crowd.

Now the attraction between them is raised to an unbearable pitch.

(five seconds, random, hickirichi)

"Have you heard that there are labor problems at the Hiroshima Munitions Works?" he asks.

(fifteen seconds, random, mokug yo)

"The most resolute discipline will have to be employed," she replies.

Now the dancer has fallen into the garden of rocks.

(one strike, densho)

"Oh! Poor man!" she cries.

(one strike, densho)

"No," he counsels, "For although he has made a fool of himself, the moon has entered the dark pattern of his heart."

Now there is an awkward silence between them.

Now the moon has entered the position called the "Dark Nipple of the Figs."

(seven seconds, random, shakuhachi)

"Oh look, the Milky Way has spread its skirts to be broken by the waves of the mountain," she cries.

(seven seconds, random, shakuhachi)

"Does it not make you feel immortal," he says, cupping her breasts, and pressing his sex against the formal pillow adorning her back.

[By Yasusada, Ozaki Kusatao, Akutagawa Fusei. Ishikawa Takuboku (1885-1912) was a militant socialist before the First World War and is one of Japan's most important tanka poets of the century. The parenthetical musical notations are entered in the hand of either Fusei or Kusatao.]

[Beginning in the 1950s' Yasusada went on to study English for fifteen years. The following piece, like the other assignments that follow, is handwritten in English and was found folded and inserted in one of the notebooks. It is graded in the upper right-hand corner as a C-. The instructor's corrections within the text have been omitted here as they have been in the other assignments we have chosen to include. There are a total of ninety nine pieces—original assignments, carbon copy letters by Yasusada, original letters written to him, and a small group of poems—that are written in English.
Ferdinand de Saussere (1857-1913) is generally regarded as the founder of modern linguistics.]

ASSIGNMENT SEVEN
April 17, 1967

It could be useful to think of the sign as coated in a covering. In that way, the thrust of the armature would, bearing its charge like a wave, conceive. We could speak of the pleasure when one comes out and goes back to the word. As if it were snow. And all the tracks left there. What the author then chooses to do is up to her. Her hair dishevelled, in stasis, or pinned-back as if travelling at a great speed . . .

There is renewed thinking now among linguists as to the definition of the sentence—a problem forgotten since its repression by Saussere. You can imagine hime *[sic, eds.]*, pacing toward the window, his fine skeletal structure revealed by the patroleling *[sic]* light. "Ah," one can imagine hime *[sic]* saying and massaging the bolt in his hand, "So this is ash," as if it were something that Akiko had done, pounding her fist to her chest and calling for Nomura, "That does it! I'm throwing away your memorium *[sic]*!" and thus on . . . Or, "Small particles of meaning satisfy this best for the writer; though large structures do so, openly, they do so as structures . . ." In thus a way the word "skye"*[sic]* could be a sentence or a wave, Nomura covered in ash, travelling at a great speed, toward an armature that is swelling. Into which, thus, an adolescent forme *[sic]* has been hammered.

[Note from English teacher at bottom of page]

Mr. Yasusada: This is most interesting, though I honestly fail to see any connection whatsoever to the assignment. There are a number of syntactical miscues, and I am puzzled by the obvious spelling errors, which one hardly expects from an advanced student like yourself. Mr. Davies, with whom I have shared this, agrees. I am wondering if you have heard of the writer James Joyce, who is famous for a form of writing called "streams *[sic]* of consciousness?" I must say that this makes me think of him! Are Saussere, Nomura and Akiko real people, or characters you have invented in a flight of fancy? In any case, we will meet for refreshments at the Cultural Institute, as planned, on Tuesday at 3pm. Until then,

Mr. Rogers

[This undated piece was discovered folded and inserted in a copy of Kawabata Yasunari's The Snow Country, *found among Yasusada's belongings. In a hurried, penciled script, it is written in English, with the exception of the interjections from the* Tosa Diary*, which are copied in Japanese on a separate, attached page, and accompanied by indications as to where they are to be inserted in the "diary entry." We have placed these passages into the text accordingly, using the English translation of the scholar G.W. Sargent. We have indicated these in italics, although we would stress it is not clear whether Yasusada intended the* Tosa *passages to appear in Japanese or in English. In addition, as per the directions of Yasusada's heading note, we have reprinted, verbatim, all writing under erasure in the original. The "title" preceding the entry suggests that Yasusada may have intended this as part of a longer fictional series, although this is the only example of its kind among the material presently in our hands.*

Rita Hayworth is perhaps best known for her titillating pin-up photograph, much displayed throughout the barracks of the U.S. Armed Forces during World War II. According to the book, The Story of English *(ed. McCrum, et.al., 1986), a crude likeness of this photograph was painted onto "Little Boy," the device dropped upon Hiroshima. How Yasusada had apparent knowledge of this fact we do not know. The top margin of the first page contains Yasusada's jottings on times and dates for various appointments, but these are not reproduced here.]*

[Yasusada notes]   (for From the Diary of Rita Hayworth)
            (and keep cross-outs in diary entry)

DEAR DIARY:

Diaries are things written by men, I am told. Nevertheless I am writing one, to see what a woman can do. What an incredible ~~day~~ night and day it ~~was~~ has been today! Clark called at 10 just as Teofilo (he still can't get the macaroni *al dente!*) brought breakfast and ~~it~~ my heart soared beyond the clouds. *We offered up prayers for a calm and peaceful voyage—"all the way to Izumi Province." Fujiwara no Tokizane arranged a farewell celebration "for the road" (not very appropriate for a ship, perhaps) at which everyone, from master to servant, became disgustingly drunk.* Why is it that only a few moments can turn ~~the darkness~~ the darkness that has ~~followed~~ enshrouded my soul into the very brightful [*sic*, eds.] day? *As the full moon grew faint in the morning sky, the provincial overseer of religion arrived to give us a farewell blessing. Every one, high and low, old and young, was fuddled with drink. Even people who have never learned to write the figure one were merrily dancing figures of eight.*

Does he desire me in a true way? Oh, I know ~~his~~ the stories about it might not be so, and probably it is only a passing fancy on his parts [*sic*]. Still, it is possible to dream, and the dreaming does do me good. Oh, Clark (sigh). *Oh I will never forget your countenance as we passed the pine-covered beaches of Uta. Pines beyond number! How many tens of centuries have they stood there? Waves wash the roots of each tree, and from each topmost branch a crane soars into the air.*

Speaking of dreaming, dear diary, I dreamed last night of ~~falling~~ being painted like a ~~cartoon~~ whore onto metal and falling for a long way through ~~the~~ some far-off air. I was crouching like a cat or like a toad, and my nipples were hard and ~~long~~ large as ~~thumbs~~ peppers!!! ~~That~~ This was how I had been painted by the hand of I never will know who. I felt as if I were ~~not my body~~ emprisoned *[sic]* within a body that was not my own but was, in the end, my ~~own already~~ finally true body. (I must relate this tomorrow to his Holiness Swami Ravadanada.) *The mountains and sea grow dark. Soon it becomes impossible to distinguish east from west.*

And then I woke up. Oh diary, there are times when I feel that my facilities are just going wild with haywires! *[sic]* ~~The script from Houston is~~ And I just can't seem to get myself to ~~pick up~~ study that ghastly script about ghosts. I'm such a procrastinator. ~~I wish think sometimes I could just die!~~ Having no excellence within myself, I have passed my days trying to make special impressions on everyone. Especially the fact that I have no man who will look out for my future makes me actually feel sick to ~~my stomach~~ myself! *[sic]* I don't want to bury myself in dreariness, but in the end, the courtesan on this Japanese screen seems more real than me. I imagine I ~~join~~ become her sometimes, and on moonlit nights in autumn, when I am hopelessly sad, I often go out on the balcony and gaze dreamily at the moon. It makes me think of days gone by. Teofilo says that it is dangerous to look at the moon in solitude, but something impels me, and sitting a little withdrawn I muse there. In the wind-cooled evening I play on my mouth-harp, though others probably wouldn't care to hear it. I feel that my playing betrays my sorrow, which with the music becomes ever more intense, and I become disgusted at myself—so worthless and pathetic am I!

I feel my pulse when the heart-skip strikes. And when I lift my arms to examine my breasts, I just can't help ~~count the~~ but count the pimples under my arms. Who invented shaving, anyway? Nine on the left, five on the right. And today, dear diary, I have an important announcement to make: I have resolved that on my birthday, nine months from today, I will give up alcohol forever, ~~and~~ only drinking champagne, wine or ~~sherry~~ sherry on the most special of occasions, and never, never under any circumstances, when I am alone. *From now on we row farther and farther out to sea. It is for this reason that all of these people have gathered here to see us off. Little by little, at every stroke of the oars, the watchers standing by the shore slip away into the distance, just as we on the boats, too, grow more*

72

and more indistinct to them. On the shore, perhaps, there are things they would like to say to us. On the boats there are things we would like to convey to them—but to no avail.

~~Well~~ Well, I am sleepy now. Will Clark call again tomorrow? Life is so full of surprises, and tomorrow when I awake and the morning sun and the blue birds ease through the gauze of my dreams, it ~~will~~ shall be the first day of the rest of my life! ~~And yet And yet~~ As we reach the house and pass through the gate, everything stands out brightly under the clear moon. Things are even worse than we feared—there is a wilderness of decay and desolation. It looks as if in a moment's passing, a thousand years of suffering have left their mark here... There are many things which we cannot forget, and which give us pain, but I cannot write them all down. Whatever they may be, let us say no more. Dear diary, I bid you good night!

*[The Tosa Diary (circa 936) describes the return of a governor of Tosa province to Kyoto. Tosa province is the ancient name for the present Kochi Prefecture on Shikoku Island. While the diary is categorically presented as written by one of the ladies in the party, there is general consensus among scholars that the author is nonother than the governor himself, the legendary poet Ki no Tsurayuki. At the bottom of the page, Yasusada has copied, in black ink (and apparently sometime subsequent to the composition of the "diary entry") the following quote in the original French from Tzvetan Todorov's Theories du symbole: "[the symbol] achieves the fusion of contraries; it is and it signifies at the same time; its content eludes reason: it expresses the inexpressible. . . . the symbol is produced unconsciously, and it provokes an unending task of interpretation. . . . in the symbol, it is the signified itself that has become a signifier; the two faces of the sign have merged."]

[undated]

Returning
to the shadows of the blossoms
the shadow of another life

[undated]

In the abbot's voice
the shape of a mountain
has appeared

May 3, 1967

SUITOR RENGA*

You are the most beautiful girl in Hiroshima, and I am the suitor.

Around the stone the irises are moist and lascivious.

Although the suitor written above does not exist.

Nor are there traces of suitors left in Hiroshima to speak of thus.

Even when flower-bearing (even when a passerby cries, "Oh, there goes a suitor") the latter is an [illegible, eds].

You are the most beautiful girl in Nagasaki and.

You are shy and wear a large pin in your hair.

Now we have come full circle and.

Don't lean too close, your eyes seem to be saying.

"The radius delimits the unnatural size of the flowers."

You are running like a sprinter with a bluish bubble on your back.

Now we have arrived in the area of the white blossoms.

You are a little girl with blistered face, pumping your legs at a great speed beside the burning form of your Mother and.

Now we have arrived in the area of the white blossoms.

"And now darling," says the tourist, "have we come to the long slate-bed of Kamakura suitors?"

A suitor emerges joyous from the meeting, for he has conquered shyness by assuming [illegible] mannerisms.

*[By Yasusada, Ozaki Kusatao, Akutagawa Fusei.]

75

[undated]

In the temple's silence
shaped like a hammer
the hammer's silence

[*Yasusada note*] Assignment 20 ("Writing in the style of another")
May 21, 1967

The Poet Receives a Card of Congratulations from His Ex-Wife Upon the
Publication of His First Booke. [sic., eds.]

Your poems are very beautiful, so pure
and classical in voice and tone; the mythylogicol [*sic*]
allusions in contemporary context daring
yet precise. Astonished, a friend of mine likened
your resonance to that of Catullus. I am in love
with those lines that open the ode on Persephone:

That hair curled with hot irons,
drenched in myrrh, Turnus is driven
at high speed by the Furies . . .

Who could ever know that behind such a voice,
is the heart and soul of an asshole?

Mr. Rogers: May I explain? Your assignment of writing in the voice of
another is followed here, but in a libertarine [*sic*] way. In fact, what I
have done here is to provoke a *triple* imitation: Here are the voices of 1)
the wife, 2) the poet, and in echoes (so I hope) of 3) Catullus, the great
erotic poet of the Empire of Rome. You kindly asked us to write in the
voice of another. I believe, very frankly, that all writing is quite already
passed through the voices or styles of many others. This, I believe in my
heart, is the very marrow of writing.

Yasusada

[*Note from English teacher at bottom of page*]

Dear Mr. Yasusada:

I would strongly disagree with your observations about "writing" (oth-
erwise, how could we account for those authors of the past who have
displayed unquestionable originality and greatness?). After all, are
Homer, Shakespeare, or Sir Walter Scott, say, one of the great poets of
my own land,* "passed through the voices of others"? If you think so, I
would be very interested in hearing your argument! Nevertheless, I am
pleased to give you an "A" for unusual imagination and creativeness.
And, I should say, for your rather wicked humor as well!

Mr. Rogers

*[*This reference reveals that Mr. Rogers was Scottish.*]

November 7, 1967

Dear Fusei:

Kuribayashi returned from San Francisco a few days ago. It is sad, but his father died while he was there. Of course, he had been very ill, and Natsume [Kuribayashi, eds.] is grateful he was able to be with him in his last days.

I have found out, as well, more sad news: Jack Spicer died only a short time before I wrote my first letter to him more than two years ago.[1] Apparently he drank quite heavily, and died as a result of this. While that tragically explains why I never had response from him, it *is* strange that the publisher never wrote me back, considering that three letters were sent.

In any case, you will be happy to know that Kuribayashi brought back another book by Spicer, with the title *After Lorca*. I discovered through some research at the library that Federico Garcia Lorca is an important poet of Spain, who was shot by fascists in 1936. Unfortunately, no one has apparently yet translated him (the only modern Spanish poet in Japanese that I have come across is a philosopher named Unamuno[2]— and not all that interesting). Someone *should*, as you will be able to tell after reading Spicer's versions. It is a very strange collection, containing not only the translations, but a formal correspondence (there are five letters) from Spicer to the dead poet! The letters are very beautiful, and full of the bizarre, yet very careful, twists and turns we have so admired in *Billy the Kid, Language,* and *The Heads of the City [sic] Up to the Aether.* And to add to the delight, there is an introduction to the book by Lorca written from the grave!

I am so taken by the conception of the book, that I have decided to correspond with Spicer in a like manner. I do feel that certainly, were he alive, he would have written back to me and that a friendship might well have ensued. After I finish, I will allow him the opportunity to introduce the collection with the same generosity of spirit that he extended to Lorca. What do you think?[3]

Kusatao and I will wait to hear from you regarding dates for your visit next month. Besides Spicer, there are interesting new books here waiting for you by poets named Gary Snyder, Bob Kaufman, Kenneth Rexroth, Howard McCord, Robert Creeley, Helen Adams [sic], and Lawrence Ferlinghetti. Kuribayashi tells me that they were strongly recommended to him by McCord, the owner of City Lights Bookstore, a popular bookseller in San Francisco.[4]

A warm greeting to you and family!

Yasusada

(P.S. There is also a very interesting looking book by one Roland Barthes, entitled *Empire of Signs,*[5] which I haven't yet had time to read.)

[1. See letter of November 17, 1965.
2. Miguel de Unamuno, leading philosopher and theoretician of the early Spanish modernist movement.
3. If these letters were ever written, they do not appear in the fourteen notebooks that we have. It is possible that carbon copies of them were inserted into a notebook lost in transit from Japan which had not been fully reviewed before its disappearance. Indeed, this notebook contained numerous loose-leaf insertions.
4. Yasusada is confused here, as the real owner of the City Lights Bookstore is the poet Lawrence Ferlinghetti.
5. Given the date of this letter, Yasusada could only have had the original French version. Indeed, according to his son, he had an advanced reading proficiency in this language.]

[undated] *
>—I dedicate this poem to the great American poet, Jack Spicer

Built of porous sound. The temple beyond this in the chrysanthemums
and Hiroshima pinegrounds. Out of focus. A temple where we measure
silence.

Hear not through thus this was not possible with love but in beginning
not to be a human being. Thus toward beginning not to be a symbol.

A symbolic worshiper. Thus words are sounded so so they burn
in the worshipers soul. Or Hiroshima. A signed gap for the passerby.

Where one is is in a temple which yes makes us forget
that we are in it. Where we are is in a silence.

Where we are this is curious. Where we are a dream of transparent
letters blocks the heart from suchness which is not. Thus this is precise-
ly where we are we are not to meet.

* *[Given the last "sentence," it would seem most likely that this imitative poem was
written after Yasusada was informed of Spicer's death. As well, it may have been
intended as part of a series Yasusada alludes to in his letter to Fusei of November 7,
1967. The original is written in English.]*

6 *

You turn on and off, and
If I pass my tongue through your speaking mouth, I know that there
   is nothing there. But if I hold my tongue inside a written
   sentence,
It blisters.
This is an act of forgetting that the dead are dead and that is
   that. Forgetting the candle held behind the figure speaking
Behind the screen.
Or does the mouth, calligraphic friend, cast its own shadows?
   "At Hiroshima," you write, "the shadows of the victors were as if
   photographed into concrete building blocks."
Or are they just turned on for a long time? Or do we two share a
forgotten tongue?
Or do they funnel us both to the ideograph barely legible on the paper
   screen—
The space around it
Where the shadow and the mouth are one?

*[In ink calligraphy in katakana syllabary on handmade paper looseleaf. This poem is a
transformation of poem #6 in Jack Spicer's 1965 collection Language. The direct quote
from Spicer's original contains a variant: Yasusada has brushed "victors" for "victims".]

April 9, 1968

SENTENCES FOR JACK SPICER RENGA*

Walking, we insisted the Manyoshu was a blur, and why we said it on that path is also a blur.

(seven beats, rapidly, ko-tsuzumi)

The tile has a pattern and a dancer walking there.

(rrrr went a bell, and the dancer went rrrr)

The lover was like a rose, beneath the light of the bar, leaning.

Going out and into the shadows that are massed against the sound of a bell.

(one strike, densho)

You wouldn't believe what the others said:

(five seconds, random, shakuhachi)

They said things like "Death," "Yukio Mishima," or "Have a nice day."

(five seconds, random, hickirichi)

The lover lay down on the stone and I pulled off my shirt or vice-versa.

(ten seconds, random, da-daiko, uckinarashi, mokug-yo)

There were flowers, flattened, in the closed book.

Alias, I said, I quote you.

(one strike, densho)

Alias, the book is near your ear, in the photograph that is about you.

(one strike, densho)

(His seems to be a "heady" sort of writing, in love with the trace of thought itself)

So the writing is barely legible on the ancient screen.

(seven beats, rapidly, ko-tsuzumi)

So I call back his arm, drifting into the massed shadows of the rose.

(one strike, densho)

Now the dancer is tracing a pattern over the pattern, feet clicking against the tile.

[By Yasusada and Akutagawa Fusei.]

[Ink-brushed notes added below in Fusei's calligraphy]

No messages, no intention to share emotion. No lyrical intensity— percussive soundings within patterns of harmonic or dissonant chords; utterance as autonomous fact *and* its saturation in context (*this* tension). Gaps as intrinsic to such grammar—less as caesura than as sign. Spicer's ghost as a concave form I glimpsed, hovering, a few feet above poem.

[Yasusada's cursive note added in pencil] Ask Mr. Davidson[1]: What does he think that word truly means—"lyrical." And ask him also, what is the meaning of those broom-like forms attached to the front of his skirt?

[1. From material in the notebooks we know that Mr. Davidson was a teaching colleague of Mr. Rogers, and, like the latter, a native of Scotland. From this and other notes in the notebooks, it appears that these individuals sometimes wore their native costumes while teaching.]

ASSIGNMENT #29

(Write a paragraph describing yourself with substance, sincerity, and accuracy. The paragraph should exhibit the qualities of unity, order, completeness, and coherence as we have discussed them in class.)*

Biographical Note

Araki Yasusada translates with *accuracy* from six languages: French, English, Canadian, Australian, Zelandish, and Korean. One day, in the revolving restaurant, he was served a large platter of fuku,* arranged in the form of an exultant swan. Chewing on this he thought about himself. He is a widower, and lives in the prefecture of Nara, which after reconstruction, has become uncommonly picturesque. What the writer means by "picturesque," of course, is purely in the mind of the beholder. The man across from him (who bore an uncanny resemblance to himself [to the writer, that is]), exhibited a calligraphic figure cut into his brow which, with each bite, became progressively filled with transparent beads. May I have, he said, in a perfectly *sincere* voice, something with which to wipe myself? Thus, the ivory sphere was hidden away in a part of the turning room that was not a part of the turning room. I'm inclined to forget about these things, he said, like Shixes himself, when the theft has become a part of the very *substance* of me. He has been a postman since 1927, and delivers the mail. He is what they call a "Hibakusha."

[English instructor's note at page bottom] Mr. Yasusada: Please see me after class.

[The heading is mimeographed. One of 54 English writing assignments found in the notebooks. The three italicized words are underlined in the original. Fuku, or blowfish, is mortally poisonous if even a tiny trace of its liver is consumed. The diner, then, always takes his chances that this coveted delicacy has been properly prepared by the chef.]

HORSEHIDE AND SUNSPOT
July 17, 1968
-Hiroshima Municipal Stadium-

Chalk-lines, in sun, extend themselves infinitely.

Cleat-tracks and *[illegible, eds.]* engrave the paths ephemerally.

(Also, horsehide and pinewood are soundless and.)

Thus now Carp and Sparrows* tense their tiny bodies and leap hither.

On the diamond where a temple once stood.

As seventy thousand voices are fused by a sphere and.

*[along margin, written horizontally] Don't forget sake for Shimpei**

A corolla of screams ringing absence is viscerally real.

And so, like a sunspot, is baseball.

[Hiroshima Carp and Yamaguchi Sparrows, Major League baseball teams of Japan. The poem is written on the back of a scorecard. Kusano Shimpei (1903-) is a major avant-garde figure in Japanese poetry and was an acquaintance of Yasusada, Kusatao and Fusei.]

[undated]

Turning the sutra page—
a light is shining
far back in the trees

Silk Tree Renga*

[undated]

Happening to notice the willow leaves in the garden, a braille page of words

The voices of the sorority girls sing of fucking in a plaintive way

Dressing their frail bodies in armor are the young widows of the prefecture of

It was there we saw the trace ruins of an ancient dog-shooting range

So running after me was the young child whose name is Manifold

A screen of moonflowers and creeping gourds, with a thicket of cockscomb and goosefoot, evoking cocks and cunts

She told me then that the master of the house had left for a certain location in town and that I had better look for him there pronto, if I desired to speak to him

Everybody was fucking overjoyed to see him, as if he had returned from the dead

Terrified by these words he walked straight into the province of Kaga

How Ungo's sitting rock is still there after all these years

Where patches of lichen have flowered over glyphs

On the third day he drew a figure, and inside of it a detailed map of the pampas moor of Mano

Was it male or female? He loved to make them guess whether the stroke in that place was a cock or a cunt

More and more he became obsessed with the seedling form of this great pine in the time of ancient gods

Thus during sitting, he had felt the Milky Way as a pair of thongs between the toes

There were countless boats, large and small, anchored in the
deep harbor

He dreams of a gigantic mountain, shaped like the word which names it

There are manifold trees and plants which rise from it, saplings and
great trees and plants beyond words or morphemes

Why don't you go fuck yourself, she said, throwing the thong at his
head and missing

I was reminded then of the priest Noin, who had wept to find on his
return visit the same tree cut and thrown into the Natori River as bridge
piles by the new governor of the prefecture of

So nothing there was moistened with meaning

In fact, in the very gesture of the geisha, was the retreat of a whole
genre

So that Mount Chokai was made invisible on the watery beach of
Shiogoshi

Or turned upon the sand into the shape of a flowering silk tree

Thus the interiors of two sacred structures of whose marvels I had
heard with unbelieving ears were revealed to me

*[By Yasusada, Ozaki Kusatao, Akutagawa Fusei. Some lines in this renga (if in modi-
fied form) have their source in Matsuo Basho's great haibun diary, Narrow Road to
the Interior.]

[The following brief prose pieces were found entered in English at various places in the last notebook. Because each bears a check mark in green ink above it, they appear to have been intended to be grouped. The references to Marcel Duchamp and to the American conceptual artist Robert Smithson are quite interesting, and we believe Yasusada must have been exposed to their work through his contact with the artists of the Gutai (see letter on p. 25-26). In addition, it will be noted that "What is the diffirince," is composed of famous quotes from the American poet Gertrude Stein and the French Surrealist painter Margritte.]

A FRAME

So placing the frame over the piece of writing he said, "do you not think that knowing to look at all is rather a lot?" And then he looked within that and wrote out of it.

WHAT IS THE DIFFIRINCE?*

Is a rose is a rose is a rose the same as Ceci n'est pas une pipe?

*[The misspelling is in original]

Conceptual Essay

What or where is "The Estate of Robert Smithson"?

Savage Literatus

Then the killer woke up in the sentence, the spurs still spinning on his wrists: Phew, he said in demotic, it was only a dream.

Some Time

Now is writing, Gwintir, my prince, *ever* in the past?

DUCHAMP'S DISSERTATION

—for Takiguchi Shuzo *

It is a book. And I have found it.

*[Takiguchi (1903-1979), an artist and critic, was Japan's leading scholar on the work of
Marcel Duchamp. We do not know if he and Yasusada had a personal acquaintance with
one another.]*

[Untitled and undated, these haiku—all containing the word "against"—are present in various pages of one of the notebooks. Although their projected final configuration is uncertain, they appear to have been intended for, or as, a series, as each has been checked with a red pencil mark. They are presented in the sequence of their appearance. It does appear to us that these pieces unmistakeably bear the stamp of the famous poet, and Holocaust survivor, Paul Celan. Although there is no record in the notebooks of Yasusada's familiarity with Celan, it is known, from Ogiwara Seisensui's writings, that his work was read by the Layered Clouds group and critically discussed by them.]

Dwarf-birches: in film, against the shadows, it is spring

Slit-chisel: the long passage is against the mantis-pulse

Poppy-capsule: splitting in the breast, against the parting of a daughter

Star-group: against sorrow, rice gathering

Gravel-club: amulet pressed against the absence of the mason

Chalk-crocus: lining the river, mouths blooming against nature

Scratch-sheets: against the whiteness, the rough root-skin

Shell-urn: ceaselessly, against itself

Prayer-silo: against its wall, the unborn in pattern

Grief-stone: rubbed against flesh, *[illegible, eds.]* sky expectant

Cross-beam: against it, in the koan, a swarm of starlings to unravel

[undated]

Faint memory
of her lithe body—
wet smacking
of the mud snails

[Undated and in English. Yasusada note at top of passage]
(When reading out loud, read in voice of American cowboy actor.)*

Nope, the periphery of her experience was no greater than the mountainous terrain surrounding the actor...

And then the noematic core of her perception shifted; if she would not soon become that cactus, the hand which had settled like a bird on her thigh would penetrate her being like a crazed piston.

[While there are numerous marginal or uncontextualized notes like this in the notebooks, we enter this one because it is suggestive of an interest Yasusada seems to have had in the American West. Indeed, there is a series of Japanese sound-play poems in one of the notebooks, "spoken" by the American cowboy actor Gene Autrey (into which this passage is arrowed as an English interjection) which are completely untranslatable.]

[undated]

Spring has come—
a grub goes burrowing into blossoms
on a cylinder grave

[undated]

A mud snail crawls—
in the world, sorrow and happiness
undulate, undulate

[The following typed letter was found in one of the notebooks among returned English class assignments. The carbon copy of Yasusada's reply, which follows here, was attached to it with paper clip.]

Friday 11

Dear Mr. Yasusada:

By now, there is no reason for me to be guarded in my words. I have now confessed, if most ungraciously, all of my feelings for you. I request your forgiveness for the embarrassment and discomfort my candor surely caused you. I want to thank you for the gentleness of your reproach, and to tell you that I want, as much as possible, for our relationship to continue along the lines of friendship and professional respect it had enjoyed until last night at the Tosho-ri. I don't presume to ask that you forget the indiscretions of my behavior, only that you accept my sincere desire to be your friend, and—from my deep respect for the greater creative powers you evince—that you allow me to continue as your teacher of English.

May all this be, purely, a matter between us? The purity of spirit I have been graced to see in you, makes me confident that it will remain so.

Your friend,

Mr. Rogers

July 12, 1968

Dear Mr. Rogers:

Yes, why should this all not remain, purely, between us? One's desires in this world, it seems to me, are of a small consequence. Why feel badly about them?

The sparrow paces on the tatami mat; the wind sounds in the pines.

And please, do not worry too much about my feelings. I am a rather tough but sensitive bastard who simply happens to long for the company of women (and between you and me, preferably for those who say provocative things in the heat of passion!).

And I am grateful that you have been, and always will be, my teacher of English. I ask that you look upon the elegant strangeness of this letter as an emblem of my gratitude and indebtedness to you.

Shall we have a beer soon at the Tosho-ri?

Your friend,

[signature on carbon]
Yasusada

[Undated. Given some of the poem's subject matter, we believe it dates from the 1960's or early 70's.]

—dedicated to Origuchi*

Her kisses tasted of blood, or wellwater flecked with rust?

She folded her Rose of the Snow kimono over the corner of the futon.

So you think she knew your suffering in advance?

Not knew, but represented it.

What do you mean, the right to private violence?

In her company the world was no more than the splashing water of her voice.

Do you rise like the sun over an automobile graveyard?

I wake from dreams worn out and dull as a horse.

Did you free yourself from the obligations of fidelity?

Her clinging dress always made me shiver.

What did she show you you had not already seen?

The swing phase of her walk was highly derived.

You bet on a ghost, knowing you would lose?

On the upstroke, her clavicles folded in like a jacknife.

If not in clear, distinct ideas, in what did you believe?

We were hurtling through a transparent mirror.

What did she see in the fullness of your lips?

The heartshaped impression of her clitoris.

[Origuchi Shinobu (1887-1953), novelist and critic. Both editions (1943; 1947) of Origuchi's masterpiece, Shisha no sho (Book of the Dead), *published under the pseudonym Shaku Choku, were found, heavily annotated, amongst Yasusada's belongings.*

Origuchi's fiction, traditionalist in theme, decentered in its form, and often illogical in its employments, is very much in opposition to the Western-influenced realist strategies that begin to dominate Japanese literature in the Meiji period. In fact, this opposition is explicitly dealt with in Origuchi's criticism. While there is no evidence of a personal acquaintance, Yasusada's dedication of this piece to Origuchi is thought-provoking. Indeed, Yasusada's anonymity, and the overall fragmented nature of the notebooks might be best regarded not as the incidental effects of a private diary form, but as the marks of a chosen refusal of the transplanted constructions of self that increasingly shape Japanese literature in the 20th century.]

Tirelessly, tirelessly,
moon is breathing
mountain-side lake's birth

June 23, 1968

Four Mat Room Renga*

The Taiga scroll is very beautiful, said Rikizan.

Thank you, bowed Yanagida, while kneeling in the Tendai manner.

The river runs forever in the mountains, whispered Spicer in the English language.

The carp and the water seem inlaid upon the other, growled Sekiguchi.

Then a crow was heard cawing in the pines.

Then the telescope of the old geisha was heard creaking on the other side of the paper wall.

The mouth of the concubine, replied Yoshitaka, is round and black and deep.

Thus Yanagida whisked the tea into a froth in the elaborate manner of the Onjo school.

Thus Rikizan repressed a sudden urge to release gas.

So Spicer thought to comment on Yanagida's brisk and spontaneous movements, but did not.

Then Yanagida placed the whisk beside the bowl with a click.

The whole scene was very impressive to Spicer.

Then Yanagida placed the Kamakura bowl, without a sound, in front of Rikizan.

Subsequently, Yoshitaka stood and bowed sharply to Shekiguchi.

This somewhat confused Spicer, as he had observed no apparent motive for the gesture.

Then Yanagida cocked his head suddenly toward the unexpected call of an otogisu.

Then Rikizan passed the bowl, in cross-direction, to Spicer.

The unmistakeable roar of a military vehicle was heard in the street just beyond the four-mat room.

The motion of Rikizan's passing seemed as tangible to Spicer as the cedar beam above the Taiga scroll.

Then Yanagida wiped the secondary ladle with one stroking motion.

Then he turned the black powder bowl quickly, two times.

Then Sekiguchi cleared his throat loudly in defiance of convention.

It was then that Yoshitaka noticed the silver flash of a plane high in the morning sky.

Thus, Spicer stole a glance at Sekiguchi's sipping demeanor.

Then, raising his cup, he imitated him, though rather awkwardly.

Then, Sekiguchi, noticing the compliment, drank in three rapid slurping swallows.

It was then that Spicer noticed a small, darkish stain on Yanagida's kimono.

It has the beauty of things that have seen long service, thought he.

Then a sparrow began to sing on a branch outside the sliding screen.

Thus, Spicer raised the bowl with trembling hands to his lips.

All those present smiled in profound affection for the American visitor.

[By Yasusada, Ozaki Kusatao and Akutagawa Fusei. The presence of Spicer as a participant in this iconoclastic tea ceremony is clearly an imaginative addition by the authors. It is not clear whether the Japanese participants named are fictional or actual personages.]

104

Javier del Azar
14 Oriente 614
Colonia Centro
Puebla, PUE
Mexico 72000

Araki Yasusada
3-3-16 Minami-ku
Hiroshima 734 Japan

August 12, 1969

Dear Araki Yasusada:

I hope Jose Carlos Becerra[1] will have passed on my messages. Since I received your manuscript, which I read immediately, I have wanted to write back, but for this or that reason I could not bring myself to do it. With much more time to gather my thoughts, I am now writing this letter in belated answer to your kind letter and manuscript.

I, too, wish that there had been more time to talk after the performance[2], for I realize now that I have found a brother-soul. Your work is truly all instinct and intuition, but with the fine gaze of a serpent—a gaze which sees across the pond to the other side of the river [sic, eds.]. And the imagery and statement is lavish in velocity, an impatient confluence of realities . . . But I shall leave all that for now, hoping we will be able to discuss it personally and at length sometime in the near future. Perhaps I will be able to return to Japan before too long, or, even better, perhaps you might visit me in Mexico someday. Let us discuss these possibilities further.

In the meantime, I have produced a piece of music which owes much more than its title to your endearing, yet unsettling poem, "Sarcophagus and Maracas"[3]: It involves a percussionist performing with a pair of maracas together with a magnetic tape made of pre-recorded sounds! I still don't know how the mixture will work on stage, but I hope that the primordial nature of these simple instruments, pitted against the disembodied sounds on the tape, will generate a timeless "something other". . . the kind of substance which I found so mercurially present in your manuscript. The whole experiment was more difficult than I anticipated, partly because the studio where I produced the tape was going through difficult times (they were even running out of razor blades!).

I am intending to send the material to Barry Anderson[4] in London, hoping that he'll be interested in promoting a performance, so we'll have to wait . . . But for now, I thought you should be the first to have a copy of the score[5], if anything, as a silent but pregnant symbol of my gratitude and admiration.

Yours sincerely,

[signature] Javier del Azar

[1. Typed and in English, the letter was found folded with the pages of the score in one of the notebooks. Jose Carlos Becerra was one of the outstanding Mexican poets of his generation. He died in a car accident in Italy in 1970.
2. We do not know if del Azar is referring to a performance of his own work or to something other.
3. We assume that the "manuscript" del Azar refers to is a selection of English versions from Yasusada's notebooks. While del Azar's reference to "Sarcophagus and Maracas" (see p. 42) indicates that there was a clean copy (or an even further revised version) made of the poem, only the version amended by Yasusada's hand is present in the notebooks.
4. Barry Anderson, born in New Zealand, was a composer and one of the pioneers of electronic music in Britain. He died in Paris in 1988.
5. Only the four pages reproduced here were found, and they do not appear to be in continuous sequence. We have been unable to locate any further information about the score (which reveals unusual calligraphic dexterity), and are uncertain how many pages from it are missing. Indeed, we have located no further copies of correspondence between Yasusada and del Azar, nor have we been able to find any references to a Mexican composer of such a name. The score fragments are of an extremely high originality and complexity, leading us to suspect that del Azar may be a pen name for a known composer of the period. There is a handwritten note beneath the Mexico address above, apparently by del Azar: Only until December of this year.]

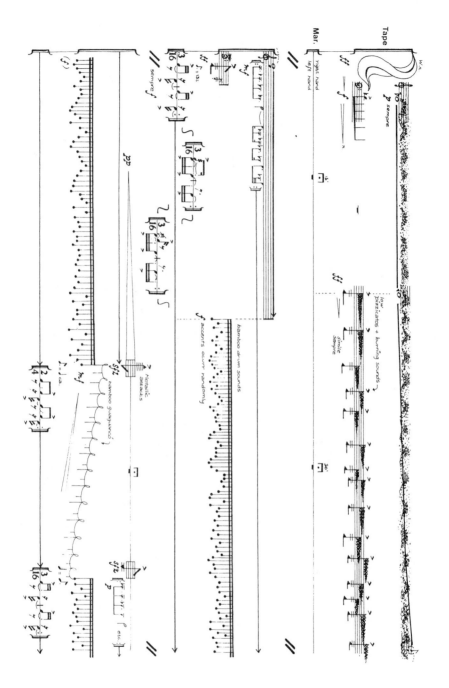

107

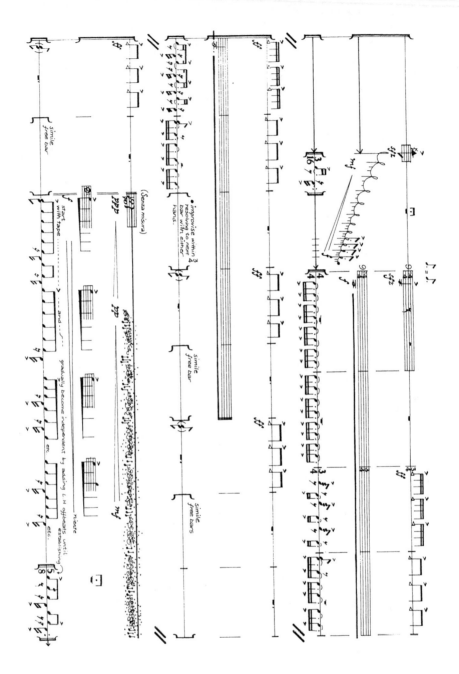

108

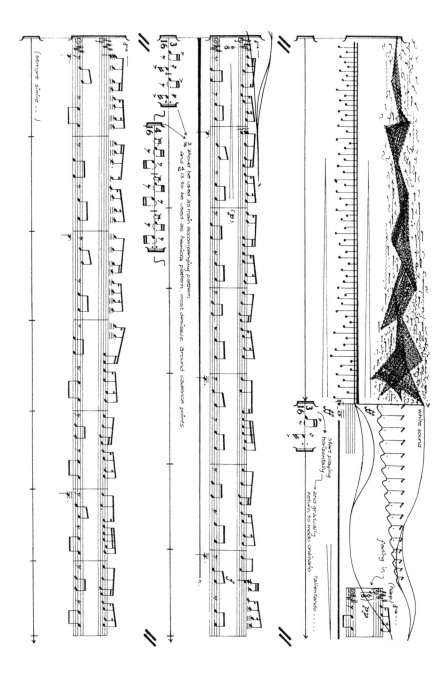

109

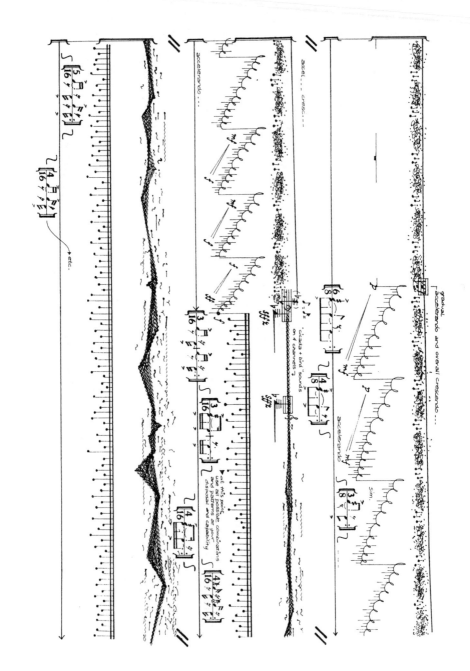

[undated]

"Astronomers working in the observatory on Mount Palomar in California, report that they have captured unprecedented images of a giant exploding star, at the distance of 25 million light years from the Earth. Such a phenomenon is known to astronomers as a 'Super Nova.'"*

Only now he orbits back to mind: blistered, sobbing boy, turning this way and that, begging for his Mother, perhaps his Father.

See him shaken off, pushed down, to fall on hands and knees; see him trampled, see him rise, sit down, half-rise, trampled.

Run, Araki, run, to make it to the river!

After 25 million years, that collapsing world still causes useless tears to fall.

[From Hiroshima's principal daily newspaper, Chugoku Shimbun, November 2, 1969. Yasusada had clipped the article about the super nova and underlined the passage quoted here. The article was found folded and inserted in one of the notebooks where the above poem is entered.]

[undated]

in the graveyard at dawn   I greet the panting runner

March 3, 1970

Where our house once stood
the pinecones have fallen
among the pinecones

SPEECH AND PUN
August 9, 1970

[Yasusada note at top of page] (When read out-loud, use Greek chorus mask—or Noh mask if none is available—and spirit-voice for parenthetical lines.)

What had no speech at ground was unspeakeably beautiful from the air.

(Form rising like a smoke-pear from the essence of the real)

And more real, really, than we. Funny, that is, the *[illegible, eds.]*, of our voices against it.

(Let us, then, Lysias, go take a tour with the tourists, of the shadows cast on the cave-wall)

Flattering, that is, to imagine the ideal bothering to descend to this ephemeral realm.

(Imagining, that is, the poison as if cure, and vice versa)

Descending, pun-like, in the name of the living.

(And that it must, repeatedly, to repeat the pun)

[Yasusada note at bottom of page]

See *The Phaedrus*, pages 262 a-b; 263-b—264-c; 272-e—274-a.

[undated]

Autumn moon—
from the monk's cell
soft weeping seeps out

February 20, 1972*

Waves of drifting snow—
my newborn son
deep in a dream

*[The poem is a reminiscence. February 20 is the birthday
of Yasusada's son, Yasunari, born in 1945.]*

March 5, 1972

Hiroshima museum—
monks whispering
near moonstones.

June 1, 1972

East of brittle ideograms
the mantis eats the mantis—
after five billion years
why not?

June 2, 1972

delicacy of delicacies
the breeze in the thick pines
of this ink-wash scroll

[undated]

—For Akutagawa Fusei (1912–1971)

I whisper and he whispers back:

no scars on faces

when moon-viewing in snow

[The following letter, undated and handwritten in English, was found folded within a copy of Kodayu Daikokuya's Dreams About Russia, *present amongst Yasusada's belongings. In its original form the letter is heavily rewritten and corrected, but the arrows and marginal notes indicating rearrangement of the passages are relatively clear, and the editors are confident that this reconstructed version is accurate. None of the other previous letters alluded to here by Yasusada appear in his manuscripts. Readers familiar with Jack Spicer's* After Lorca *will certainly find thematic and stylistic echoes of Spicer's idiosyncratic correspondence with the Spanish poet.]*

Dear Spicer:

This is the last letter. All day I have been pacing back and forth, trying to think about what this has all meant, wondering how I might say goodbye to you. I've been thinking of you writing to Lorca in a trance, of Lorca bemused by it all, sending poems to you for the sheer joy of it from the grave. Here and there, phrases from the passerby rise from the deep shade of the gingkos. Because I have lost some weight, my Father's ceremonial kimono fits me just fine. It is a very expensive one which my aunt from Kobe kept in a glass case, surrounded by tiny Shinto votives. I wish so much you could see how the cranes move deeper into the golden reeds when I bow. I watch this happen in the mirror for both of us, and the effect is rather startling. The gesture has something to do with language, but I'm not quite sure how.

It may be that that's what I heard the passerby say beneath the gingkos, and so I wrote it down.

What does it mean to write letters to a dead man, knowing that I am writing to myself? I want you to exist, I might shout into the wind. I want you to speak back to me. It may happen, at any moment, that blossoms will blow in through the open screen and be pinned for a few moments to the kimono's trees. In this transient world, who's to tell?

What you've taught me, Spicer, is that the real washes up like a dream from the unreal. Thus, when I say that on a beach against a cliff there is a boat older than Galilee, it is in the spirit of shellacking words to a page like objects to canvass. A lemon peel, a piece of the moon, two little girls playing and calling to their Father on the beach. The boat that is older than Galilee comes into the real, dragging a whole cargo of ghost-history with it. What you've taught me, Spicer, is that the unreal washes up from the real *[sic, eds.]*. Doesn't the sound of the burned one drinking from the ocean make your hair stand on end?

Now here's a thing I've been waiting until the end of our correspondence to say: You say you would like the moon in your poems to be a real moon, one that could be covered by clouds, a moon independent of images. And you say you would like to point to the moon, and that the only sound in the poem be the pointing. At first I was confused, thinking that you wanted it both ways. But now I know you mean that the pointing and the moon are one. Like these letters, for instance, which have at their heart an urn, made real by the facing gaze of two identical ghosts. An urn wrought by the moon itself and the sorrowful pointing at it. Why look any further for the real?

St. Augustine didn't, and I think that after you read this passage from his *Soliloquia* you will see reflected there an image of what your own poems desire to do. And you will see that I am in here too, gazing back at you.

> On the stage Roscius was a false Hecuba by choice, a true man by nature; but by that choice also a true tragic actor because he fulfilled his purpose, yet a false Priam because he imitated Priam but was not he. And now from this comes something amazing, which however no one doubts . . . that all these things are true in some respects . . . and that only the fact that they are false in one sense helps them toward their truth. Hence they cannot in any way arrive where they would be or should be if they shrink from being false. For how could the actor I mentioned be a true tragic actor if he were not willing to be a false Hector, a false Andromache, a false Hercules . . . ? Or how could a picture of a horse be a true picture unless it were a false horse? Or an image of a man in a mirror be a true image unless it were a false man? So if the fact that they are false in one respect helps certain things to be true in another respect, why do we fear falseness so much and seek truth as such a great good? . . . Will we not admit that these things make up truth itself, that truth is so to speak put together from them?

I know that you know there's no map for this, no destination, in our facing one another, to seek. What remains is the love in the words we move within. My daughters call, pointing to me, impatiently, on the moon-covered beach. The wind blows the blossoms in through the screen, all over the water and the trees and the cranes. Reading you, my lips move, and the urn turns, like a whole world, between us. This is where my communion with you ends and where it begins.

Now reach through, and place your hand on the papery flesh of this false face. And I shall put into my branching voice the ashy sky of your gaze.

Love,

Yasusada

BECAUSE I LIVE [1]
August 6, 1972

On this rocky slope, forty kilometers
west of Hiroshima, I am at peace.
Sachio's [2] little farm, like an amulet,
is still intact from the old days.
All day, in the pure air,
I have been reading the great poet,
Homer, in the Meiji translation of Ogai: [3]
Samurai, Surgeon General of the Imperial Army,
scholar of the Western classics, he vanished, thirty
years ago into these
pine-covered hills, without a trace.
Shiki revered him, said it was really he
who led the way back
to Buson. Old Sachio studied with Shiki,
was at his side in the last
pain-laced days. He keeps a scrap
of paper on which the Master scrawled:

I think I'll die
chewing persimmons
in the presence of peonies

It is guarded in a small box,
which he took last night
from the shelf, and opened
between us while we drank
and called back the lost faces and days.
I love Sachio deeply, and told him
so, holding his hand as he wept.

The young, wild pears on this tree
flame in the dying sun. Tonight
the names will glow quietly on the floating lamps,
and be carried out in clumps
to the sea. It is because I live
that I pluck a pear and bite
deeply into its hard
flesh. It is for them, like
the heroes of the Odyssey, rowing
rhythmically past the island of the Sirens,
that I pucker my mouth.

[1. This is the last entry in the notebooks. Yasusada died on September 29, 1972.

2. We have encountered no further mention of this figure.

3. Mori Ogai is one of the principal figures of early Japanese modernism. Yasusada's reference to Ogai's "vanishing" is curious, as it is not based in fact. Ogai had also translated Horace's De Arte Poetica. *Indeed, the rhetorical tenor of this poem seems more reminiscent of that poet than it does of Homer.*

4. Masaoka Shiki (1867-1902) and Yosa Buson (1716-1783) are regarded, along with Matsuo Basho (1644-1694) and Kobayashi Issa (1763-1827), as the greatest haiku poets of Japan. Shiki followed Buson in advocating and writing a realistic haiku based on shasei, or "sketching from real life."]

APPENDICES

APPENDICES

A FEW WORDS ON ARAKI YASUSADA AND TOSA MOTOKIYU

In the summer of 1996, after the appearance of articles in the *American Poetry Review, Village Voice,* and *Lingua Franca,* it was brought to light that the actual author of the poems, letters, and fragments of *Doubled Flowering: From the Notebooks of Araki Yasusada,* was a man bearing the pseudonym of Tosa Motokiyu. Motokiyu was our roommate in the early 1980's when the three of us were studying at the University of Wisconsin/Milwaukee, and it was during this time that he began the process of imagining Yasusada's life.

In the interview presented here, conducted with us (via correspondence and in person) by Groany McGee in early 1997, we discuss some of the background to the Yasusada writings, our roles in its presentation, and also some of the ideas and motivations behind Motokiyu's inspiration. Following the interview is a letter to Motokiyu from the distinguished Russian literary and cultural critic Mikhail Epstein. Epstein's letter arrived about two months before Moto's death, and it moved him in a deep way. It articulated, he told us, things he had intuited and would have said himself about Yasusada had he "the intellectual means." We include it here because its argument for modes of imagination and writing that transcend the conventional ways we think about authorship strikes us as very worthy of consideration. Also here is a revised and abridged version of Marjorie Perloff's widely-read essay on Yasusada published in the *Boston Review* in April of 1997 (and which was followed in the subsequent issue of the BR by invited responses from a number of prominent translators, critics, and poets). In her essay, Perloff undertakes to scratch the surface of the many obvious textual contradictions and clues woven into *Doubled Flowering* and ironically bypassed, as she points out, by the most sophisticated editors and readers—an issue we elaborate on a bit in the interview. As well, like Emily Nussbaum in her *Lingua Franca* article, Perloff proposes that the author of the Yasusada writings is "Kent Johnson," a hitherto unknown instructor of Spanish and remedial English composition. Indeed, it has been the common assumption for some time in the poetry world that Johnson is the "culprit" of the Yasusada imbroglio, though it is still inadequately explained how a community college Spanish teacher with little poetic talent could have produced work that caused fairly unbridled admiration amongst such a range of well-placed arbiters in the world of poetry.

Motokiyu, we know, would have shrugged his shoulders. Indeed, since it is clear that Tosa Motokiyu is the pseudonym of a writer with absolutely no desire to officially claim this work, why should it ultimately matter whether it is Kent Johnson, or if Yasusada's origin lies—as Mikhail Epstein surprisingly and rather convincingly proposes in his essay, "Commentary and Hypotheses"—in the prominent Russian writers Andrei Bitov and/or Dmitri Prigov? Or even, perhaps, were it to come to light, in a more stunning and unsettling authorial tale?

In any case, there is no question that in his brief life Araki Yasusada has become the most complex, discussed, and controversial case of pseudonimity in the history of United States poetry. Perhaps the articles and commentary that follow will help to make it clear that this quality of mystery should not be regarded as an incidental or distracting element of Yasusada's writing, but rather as the deep and proliferating source of its import and being.

—*Kent Johnson and Javier Alvarez*
Freeport/London
June, 1997

Why have you agreed to be the front men for the "unnamed American poet "?

Tosa Motokiyu, who had presented himself over the course of five years as the lead translator of the poems and letters of Araki Yasusada, passed away in London in the early summer of 1996. Recently, through pieces appearing in the *Village Voice, American Poetry Review* [*APR*], and *Lingua Franca*, it has been acknowledged that "Tosa Motokiyu" is the pseudonym of the actual author behind Yasusada's writings. In entrusting his works to us, Motokiyu instructed us to acknowledge publicly, after his death, that the Yasusada manuscript is a fictional creation. At the same time, he directed us never to reveal his legal name. Motokiyu was our close friend, and we had, in fact, because of his illness, been acting as liaisons for his work for over two years, submitting selections to journals, approving proofs, and handling contractual agreements. We don't then, see ourselves as "front-men," but rather as facilitators for the work of a person we loved deeply. It's our conviction that Motokiyu's work has much to say in this time when individual authorial status and self-promotion dominate most people's thinking about, and practice of, poetry.

And we would like to point out here that at no time have we stated [as was asserted by the editors of *APR*] that the Yasusada author is "American." If someone made such an assertion to the editors of the *APR*, where this was first mentioned, it was not us.

Did (or does) Motokiyu also publish work under his own name?

Yes.

In her Lingua Franca *piece, Emily Nussbaum points to Kent Johnson as "the most likely suspect" as the author of the work, citing among other things Kent's earlier publication under his own name a group of poems in* Ironwood *called "From the Daybook of Ogiwara Miyamori. You're saying, then, that this is not the case?*

That is correct. It's understandable why both of us, in fact, would be "suspected"—if one wants to use that word —since we are the only two identifiable individuals who have had unqualified access to the writing. But those who see "Kent Johnson" or "Javier Alvarez" as the "wizard behind the curtain," as Ms. Nussbaum puts it, are actually the furthest from the truth of this work, and they are the ones least able to read it with full understanding.

Did you target certain magazines, or kinds of magazines, for possible publication? If so, what were they and why were they chosen?

Yes, we sent to magazines that we thought reached important audiences in the poetry community, both here and in England. This was something

Motokiyu left mainly up to us; he was an avid reader of certain contemporary writers, but he didn't have a very close knowledge of the literary publication scene in the US and the UK.

What is the central point of the whole business? What were the primary motivations and do they still seem legitimate? Is there an aesthetic motivation for the poet, as opposed to a professional or theoretical one?

It is crucial to understand that Motokiyu is not a pen name attached to the Yasusada work after the fact. The case, rather, is that for Motokiyu the condition of anonymity was indivisible from the creation of the work. This is a crucial point to understand, especially since some readers have reacted to the work with a degree of hostility, calling the poems "hoaxes" and "fakes." But we would like to propose that if the Yasusada materials are merely "fakes," then so are the pseudonymous works of Pessoa, Pushkin, and Kierkegaard, to name just three authors who felt compelled at times to enter into other identifies in order to create. These writers wrote and published important portions of their works "as" others. For them, anonymity was not a "trick" but a need, something intrinsic to their creative drives at given times. Likewise with Moto. His fundamental motivation was to imagine another life in the most compelling way he knew how.

Thus, for Motokiyu, anonymity—and its efflorescence into the multiple names of Yasusada, his renga cohorts, and translators—was a gateway into a radically sincere expression of empathy. It's relevant here, perhaps, to offer a quote present in letters written by Moto in the year before his death to the prominent critic Eliot Weinberger and to the Nobel prize winner Kenzaburo Oe:

> (I)t's revealing, I feel, that the poetry seems to have caused the stir it has here in the U.S., even before its appearance in book form. I know that some people have questioned the legitimacy of writing in the voice of a survivor of the Hiroshima holocaust, and they seem to feel that to do so represents the appropriation of a space that a purportedly white, male, American writer doesn't have the right to occupy. Now these concerns are obviously very important, very complex, and deserving of extended thought, and I'm prepared to offer my thoughts in print should the opportunity arise. Yet it does seem relevant to raise a question here that I've often had in the back of my mind when thinking about the issue: How would those American writers who have reacted with discomfort to Yasusada react to a Japanese writer giving pseudonymous, compassionate voice to a Chinese survivor of Nanking, or to an American survivor of Bataan? Would those who have objected to Yasusada react with like negativity to such an imaginative gesture? I frankly doubt it, and the degree of unease the Yasusada has generated only registers for me how deeply a part of our lives Hiroshima and its victims are—how immediately we face them, though their faces have remained so hidden.

Exactly so —the unprecedented, and unrepeated, instance of nuclear attack that the bombings of Japan represent would seem to place them beyond the scope even of "radical" empathy. You quote Motokiyu's assertion that he was prepared to "offer his thoughts in print" about the "legitimacy" of writing in the voice of a Hiroshima survivor. Did he offer these thoughts, in print or otherwise? How did he describe the imaginative work of writing as someone who had witnessed an unprecedented form of mass violence —and the effects of this "empathy" on his own being, separate from Yasusada?

His reflections on those matters are in journal form. We will be editing some of this material for possible publication in the future.

What has been the response to the Yasusada manuscript in Japan?

No published responses that we know of yet, but the *Daily Yomiuri* of Tokyo, we hear, is planning a feature story of some kind, and we know the *Lingua Franca* article has begun to circulate and raise interest. In addition, a selection of over 50 pages of Yasusada pieces is scheduled to be published by the *Abiko Quarterly* very soon.*

Lingua Franca *cites various cases of editors being "snookered" by the Yasusada. Could you talk more about your efforts to publish the work? Were there any editors who were able to tell that the work was fictional?*

To our knowledge, no editors arrived at this position independently, through a reading of the work, even though many of the pieces contain fairly obvious hints and clues about the work's fictional status. But there were a number of editors who initially accepted the work with enthusiasm, only to reject it after hearing "the rumors"—*Harper's Magazine*, for example, along with journals in Japan and France, and two small presses in England (Spectacular Diseases and Northern House), both of which had agreed to do small books of Yasusada's poems and prose. Most notably, Jerome Rothenberg and Pierre Joris had planned to include selections from the Yasusada manuscripts in their groundbreaking anthology *Poems for the Millennium*, but changed their minds after seeing the Internet alerts. This last instance was particularly disappointing to Moto, as Jerome Rothenberg was one of his literary heroes. Moto was actually in the process of writing a long letter to Rothenberg, and in fact the draft of it was next to his bed when he died. In this draft he wonders, among other things, whether the "writing in your book only counts as innovative or exploratory if it comes accompanied with a 'certificate of authenticity?'" Now the letter is by no means as contentious as this quote might imply, but the question does strike us as legitimate.

* *In fact, a front page article on Yasusada appeared in the Asahi Shimbun, Japan's leading newspaper, on August 9, 1997.*

Is the poet going to continue to write and try to publish these (or other) poems as Araki Yasusada?

There are pieces from the Yasusada manuscript that haven't yet been published, but most of these will probably appear when the complete collection comes out. However, there are other materials in Motokiyu's papers which are fascinating, including journal writings and a fairly large body of correspondence relating to the Yasusada project. There is much to be learned about Motokiyu's thoughts and emotions therein, and we have begun to edit a selection of this work for publication.

Why was Yasusada portrayed as a Hiroshima survivor? How does the poet feel about this particular guise? Was he created in this way to make the poems more marketable?

Or is Motokiyu's work a modest gesture that confuses those demarcations of self and other that make events like Hiroshima possible in the first place? You see, Yasusada was not a "guise" for Moto, but an identity and voice that he entered in an act of transference and empathy. But the questions here are relevant and useful ones inasmuch as they imply a perceived division or incidental relationship between Yasusada's poems, fragments, and letters on the one hand, and the method of their making on the other —a misunderstanding that seems fairly widespread in terms of the work's reception, whether positive or negative. Again, for Motokiyu there was an unqualified fusion between the fictional personae and the possibility of the writing, to no less a degree, for example, than Alberto Caiero, Alvaro Campos, and Ricardo Reis are indivisible from the writing of Fernando Pessoa. Yasusada and Motokiyu: As in the illusion of the goblet and the facing silhouettes, one cannot be conceived without the other. Indeed, in work like this we are speaking about "form" as a kind of incandescence that envelopes author and persona and which confuses the usual rules we like to have for classification and for judgment.

And it is in this regard that your question of "marketability" can be turned around to ask what we think is a crucial question: To what extent are the mechanisms of the "literary market" unconsciously inscribed in the "scandal" the Yasusada has provoked? There is, after all, a very hierarchical market relationship in American poetry, involving publishers, jobs, grants, writing retreats, reading circuits, gossip mills, social events, and so on. All of this is not "incidental to the writing and its circulation and evaluation, but the very matrix within which it takes place. In short, it determines, in all sorts of subliminal ways, what counts as good. And the linchpin of it all is the function of authorship. Isn't it obvious that without secure, self-centered names to attach to works, the whole institutional edifice touched on above would simply collapse? The author of Yasusada's writings stands as a counter-example to this current order of business, one which operates as much in the circles of the "avant-garde" as it does in the "academy." That author will never be famous, will never receive any awards, job offers, or have his photograph in the leading magazines. He died knowing this would be so and wanting it that way. *Are* Doubled Flowering's *references to Barthes and Spicer meant as hints?*

Roland Barthes and Jack Spicer were two of Motokiyu's favorite authors, and they entered the fiction of *Doubled Flowering* naturally. Spicer's *After Lorca*, in fact, was Motokiyu's favorite book of poetry, and there's no question that it influenced his creation of Yasusada. Barthes's *Empire of Signs*, likewise, was a provocation. But it would be incorrect to see these authors entered into the Yasusada manuscript as "hints" about the nature of the work. Yes, there are interesting correspondences that can be found: Barthes's idea concerning the "death of the author," for example, or Spicer's notion of corresponding with the dead in *After Lorca*. But these are coincidences that we know arose without any kind of premeditated calculation. Yasusada cares about these writers because Motokiyu cared about them.

There are certainly a range of theoretical issues and problems that the Yasusada could be seen as provoking, and Motokiyu was cognizant of them and considered them deeply —issues regarding authorship, identity, evaluation, and so on. In the last month of his life, in fact, Moto received a letter from the prominent Russian philosopher and critic Mikhail Epstein, and this letter meant a great deal to him. In it, Epstein (who has published much of his philosophy under elaborate fictional identities) argues passionately for the imaginative potential of "hyper-authorship" as a mode of composition. According to Motokiyu, Epstein's letter articulated things he had intuited and would have said himself had he "the intellectual means." But it is important to understand that the formal and theoretical complexities provoked by the Yasusada are, to quote Moto again, "largely ancillary and fortuitous to the emotional impulses that have given birth to the work" His guiding desire was not to make a theoretical statement, but to imagine another life in the most original and sincere way that he was able.

Part of what disturbs editors and other readers here in the US. about the *Yasusada fiction is the wealth of "biographical" information that has accompa-* *nied the work's publication in* APR *and* Conjunctions—*including a sketch of* *Yasusada published in* APR *that replaced (and, retrospectively, seemed to lam-* *poon) the usual* APR *headshot. The information seemed supplied not only to lend* *Yasusada legitimacy as a historical person, but also as a hitherto unknown par-* *ticipant in a particular literary scene and tradition. Why the tragic details about* *Yasusada's life, his losses, and his illness?*

The details of Yasusada's personal history were not created to accompany the writing. The writing comes forth from Moto's empathic imagination of the details of Yasusada's life. Motokiyu knew all about Yasusada —his appearance, personal habits and idiosyncrasies, his literary preferences, the details of his apartment, his manner of dealing with sorrow. So there is an important sense in which Yasusada was not invented for the poems, but the poems invented for Yasusada. This is one way of understanding the meaning of the title Moto gave the full manuscript: *Doubled Flowering*. Thus, in the presentation of the poems there was no choice. Their manner of presentation was faithful to the manner of their creation, and Moto told us more than once that if he were ever to take credit for the writing that he knew Yasusada would forever cease to exist. There is no artifice in the matter. The masks are essential to the Yasusada in the same way that elaborate voicings and disguises are essential to the parallel worlds and selves that Noh actors move within. And that Moto was a great fan of Noh makes the analogy apt.

In its survey of editorial responses to the exposure of Yasusada's fictionality, the Lingua Franca piece includes a quote from APR editor Arthur Vogelsang calling the work "a criminal act," while on the SUNY-Buffalo Poetics list (where there has been quite a bit of discussion about Yasusada) one of the editors who published the work says that the "hoax" callously ignores "the pain of millions of people . . . in favor of personal gratification." How do you respond to such charges?

But isn't it the case that many important creative enterprises have been first met with anger and accusation? To us (as the editor of Wesleyan University Press honestly suggests in the same article), the strong reactions to Yasusada are further testament to the power of Motokiyu's writing and to the revolutionary promise of imagined authorship as an expressive mode. Now we are not completely certain what Mr. Vogelsang means by "criminal," but we suspect his reaction comes out of a sense similar to the comment by the other editor you mention. But it's difficult to know exactly what to say in this regard, perhaps because the very opposite seems to us so clearly the case. That is, what personal gratification, what egotistical agenda could apply here? Where is the poet who is supposedly reaping personal advantages? The Yasusada is not an egotistical gesture; it is a profoundly selfless one: a creative act of pure transference and an insistent abdication of any personal claim that might have resulted in worldly advantages. Motokiyu's absence, far from being self-centered, points toward (and we quote here from a letter he wrote to Bradford Morrow in 1995) his "desire for anonymous union with those who vanished as a result of the bombings of August 1945. To disappear, utterly, becomes a way of whispering back in the face of what is unspeakable, a manner of defying what defies representation."

The point here, partly, is that imaginative acts of transference in the context of the deeply tangled issue of Hiroshima need not—at times *cannot*—be confined to entrenched protocols of authorial closure. Clearly, the Hiroshima event haunts our collective unconscious. If one of the reasons it does so is because its transgressiveness "defies representation," isn't it understandable that the event might call forth—as one dimension of response—answerings that transgress the institutionally sanctioned codes and contracts of written expression? Not for the mere sake, that is, of being transgressive, but because working against the grain of "natural" frames of attribution and reception may offer new ways of permitting the understanding of otherness to emerge.

Those who cry foul over the Yasusada seem to feel that his imaginary life toys with the historical veracity and authenticity of a profoundly painful event. And their concerns are certainly expressed in good faith. But in the stress given to the empirical they seem to forget that empathy, commemoration, and memory are not reducible to the positivistic "accuracies" of history—for these aspects of human response are often nourished by the mythic indirectness of imagination and its elaborations. These, in turn, also become history, and add (even if in a different way than facts do) to its understanding. Araki Yasusada, the heteronymic projection of Tosa Motokiyu, himself an author who will remain forever unknown, is now an interesting, if modest, part of the complex history that emanates from the events of August 1945.

What about the question of cultural authenticity? For example, Lingua Franca *quotes John Solt, a professor of Japanese culture at Amherst, in his contention that the Yasusada "is all Japanized crap."*

Solt adds that it "plays into the American idea of what is interesting about Japanese culture—Zen, haiku, anything seen as exotic—and gets it all wrong, adding Western humor and irony. " He goes on to cite the haiku "Obediently bowing, the white flowers" and comments, "Bowing is not seen as subservient in Japan. It's a form of greeting." The comment seems to imply that a person from Japan could never bow in obedience, reverence, sorrow, what have you. Certainly Mr. Solt can't believe that an individual from Japan can only bow in "greeting." And, actually, to the extent that bowing in greeting is a cultural convention in Japan, could the gesture not be seen, precisely, as an enactment of obedience? Mr. Solt's remarks are revealing, inasmuch as in his eagerness to show how the Yasusada "gets it all wrong," he seems intent on "getting the Japanese right." A very "Western" trait if there ever was one! We would like to ask the following: Would Mr. Solt be willing to assert publicly that the primary author of *Doubled Flowering: From the Notebooks of Araki Yasusada* is not Japanese? We invite him to do so.

If Motokiyu has corresponded with Weinberger and Morrow, that would suggest several people know his real identity. Why haven't they revealed it? Has anyone announced it publicly or guessed it correctly?

Motokiyu corresponded about Yasusada with a number of people and under different pseudonyms. Will anyone "announce" his name or "guess it correctly"? Probably. But such naming games are beside the point and will be neither confirmed nor denied.

But why not? Now that Yasusada is known to be a fictional creation, why not just name his creator?

To an important extent, there can be no final answer to this question. The full motivations behind Motokiyu's insistence on an "eternal" anonymity are mysterious even to us, and there are very few, if any, parallels in poetry to such a self-effacing gesture. But here are a number of questions that might be asked in response to the question above: Why does authorial ambiguity in this instance seemingly become such a distraction or problem for so many readers? Indeed, especially now that Yasusada has been revealed to be a fictional creation—an attempt by an author of indeterminate identity to empathetically imagine another life—why is it necessary that the exact identity of that author be known? Given the fact that attributional indeterminacy is a part of the fabric of the work, why shouldn't that indeterminacy be welcomed into the very fabric of the reading experience? Why shouldn't readers be willing to abide within a kind of negative capability when it comes to the authorship of a text?

That it is so hard to accept that an author would wish to give himself over to the names of others seems to beg questions like these. And here, it seems fascinating that much of the indignant reaction to the Yasusada has apparently come from the "avant-garde" wing of the American poetry world, which in the past fifteen years or so has rather rigorously subjected the "I" and the self to theoretical critique. One could ask: Aren't heteronymic forms of authorship a promising and largely uncharted space for creative expression? Or are such forms only valid if the "I" returns to take credit for the work in the end?

Lingua Franca quotes Marjorie Perloff's opinion that "if [the editors who accepted, then rejected Yasusada] thought it was such good writing, they should still think it's good writing." Do you think this is true, or do you think that a reader's prior knowledge that she is reading a "hypernymous" author's work might engage a different aesthetic response, a different way of reading?

Yes, it undoubtedly creates a different way of reading. The question that is posed now, it seems to us, is how the work is going to be judged in its *revealed* context, i.e., the fictional writings of a Hiroshima survivor imagined by a poet who chooses in the end to sever the work from his own empirical name. Is his work good writing or not? Is it a legitimate artistic expression or not? Is it a moving form of tribute or is it merely a hoax?

You've noted that Yasusada's Japanese "translators" were part of the hypernymous complex in which the author envisioned him—organic elements, rather than mere props needed to make Yasusada a plausible fiction. Do you also see yourselves [Kent and Javier] as elements of that complex?

This is a very good question. There is a real sense, of course, in which our appearance in this work is predicated by Motokiyu's vanishing. And when the author disappears, the roles to be played by writers, readers, fictional characters, and, yes, even designated executors, become less defined and secure than they usually are.

This isn't purely accidental. Though Moto's creative energies weren't driven by theoretical concerns, we've often felt that he desired—even if the desire was mainly on an intuitive level—to create a book that was unfinished and "unbound," one where each reader's engagement with the problematics of identity and otherness inherent in *Doubled Flowering* becomes a living extension of the story it is telling. A book, in other words, not just "about" Hiroshima, but of a piece with its difficult, many-cultured, and unfolding emotional history.

The answer, then, is yes. We, too, sometimes feel like characters within a fictional dynamic that unavoidably spills beyond the pages of Yasusada's imaginary life.

Dear Tosa Motokiyu:

Thank you for your letter and rich materials that I will certainly go through with great interest.* I've been so inspired by some of your suggestions that I don't want to delay my response.

Why couldn't we establish an *International Society* (or Network) *of Transpersonal Authorship*? We could invite for membership those people who feel themselves overwhelmed by different (and multiple) authorial personalities that want to be realized through their transpersonal creative endeavors. This writing in the mode of otherness is not just a matter of pseudonym, but rather of *hypernym*. We don't produce our own works under different names but we produce works different from our own under appropriate names.

This is the crucial issue of contemporary theory and practice of writing. Poststructuralism has pronounced death sentence for the individual author(ship), but does this mean that we are doomed to return to the pre-literary stage of anonymity? One cannot enter twice the same river, and anonymity in its postauthorial, not pre-authorial, implementation will turn into something different from folklore anonymity. What would be, then, a progressive, not retrospective, way out of the crisis of individual authorship? Not anonymity, I believe, but *hyperauthorship*.

There is so much talk about hypertexts now . . . But what about hyper-authors? This question has not been even raised. Hyper-authorship is a paradigmatic variety of authors working within one (allegedly one) human entity. Hyper-author relates to an author similarly to how hyper-text relates to a text. Hypertext is dispersed among numerous virtual spaces that can be entered in any order, escaping any linear (temporal or causal) coherence. Hyper-authorship is dispersed among several virtual personalities which cannot be reduced to a single "real" personality. As thinking is always thinking "of," without necessary specification of the object, writing is always "writing by," but this "byness" of writing cannot be reduced to any biological, or historical or psychological subject. In the traditional literary theory, the author is a real individual or a group of individuals, but this is an outmoded way of thinking which can be compared with the conceptual framework of physics before the advent of quantum mechanics. The latter showed that we cannot pinpoint a particle with any specific location and time, it is a fuzzy phenomenon, embracing the aspects of discreteness and continuity, a particle as well as a wave. What I am discussing now is precisely the concept of "fuzzy," or "continuum-like" authorship, which is not a discrete personality but rather a wave, going across times, places and personalities. Tosa Motokiyu and Araki Yasusada are some of the observable locations of this hyper-authorial wave which can reach the shores of other epochs, countries, and strange personalities. Hyper-authorship is a virtual authorship in which real personalities become almost illusionary, while fictional personalities become almost real. This "almost" is what allows them to co-exist on a par in the imagination of the readers. Leo Tolstoy said: "In art, the "almost" is everything." This concerns not only the matter of artistic representation, but also the mode of authorization.

The hyper-authorship is a necessary step in the development of the theory of difference in the direction of "self-differentiation." I differ from myself in many ways, and authorship is the sphere where I create numerous "selves" different from my own. What is at stake in the contemporary issue of authorship is not creating new texts but creating new authors. The task of the author is to authorize new authorships, to proliferate authorial personalities. I ask a contemporary writer how many authors has he authored, and if none, the major point is missing.

Previously the author was interesting to a degree his/her personality could illuminate the text and be instrumental in its understanding. This tendency culminated in the widely announced "death of author" by virtue of which text became a self-sufficient and self-enclosed entity. Now I am inclined to think that text is interesting as much as it is manifesting the multiple, infinite possibilities of its authorship. What we should enunciate, perhaps on behalf of several authors, like Tosa Motokiyu, Yakov Abramov, Araki Yasusada, Ivan Solovyov, and Mikhail Epstein, is the resurrection of authorship after its death, this time in the wavy, misty, radiant flesh of prolific hyper-authorship, no more coinciding with the mortal animal flesh of a separate biological individual.

We have moved far beyond the concept of biological parenthood which is now recognized as only one of many forms of parenthood. Now let's have done with the reductive concept of authorship as only "biological" authorship limited by the input of the author as a living individual. There are many sorts and degrees of nonbiological authorship—psychological, intellectual, inspirational, magical. The question is how to differentiate these numerous authorships related to a single piece of writing, without hierarchical subordination of one to another. In what sense and in what respect Yasusada's pieces are authored by Tosa Motokiyu and Motokiyu's pieces are authored by Araki Yasusada? This is the adequate way to question the post-individual or transpersonal authorship, not just to ask: who is the real author of this work, Motokiyu or Yasusada?

The theory of difference so far has led to many unsatisfactory results, such as deadening of differences in natural origins, such as predetermined ethnic and sexual identities provoking ideological wars among their representatives. The basic contradiction of postmodern theory is between the emphases on (cultural) difference and (racial, ethnic, and sexual) identity. Why writing should be just an instrument in the assertion of one's identity, belonging to a set of natural determinants, such as race, ethnicity, gender, and sexual orientation? Writing is a challenge to my identity whence the series of hyper-authors proceed, different from the biological author and from one another. Writing would be the imaginative erasure and transgression of origins rather than their ideological reinstatement. Writing would be a progression of difference in my relationship with myself—and by the same token my increasing involvement and integration with others.

Isn't Yasusada a mark of your difference from yourself, as well as the mark of your "transcultural" involvement with Japanese culture, Hiroshima experience, etc.? The next step in the theory of difference will be to foreground what is different from difference itself. Difference, to be what it is, must be increasingly different from itself. The difference between me and non-me is only the first, naive form of difference which in its maturation turns into the difference between me and me and, therefore, grows into the expanded identity of "me and the other," thus giving rise to a new order of integrity, non-totalitarian totality. One way to push difference beyond difference is the multiplication of authorial personalities under the category of hyper-authorship.

There is a principal asymmetry and disproportion between living and writing individuals in the world. It's evident that not all living individuals have inclination and capacity to become authors. This renders quite plausible the complementary statement: not all authors have inclination and capacity to become living individuals. There are many authors who, for some reasons (which need further exploration), have no potential for physical embodiment, as there are many individuals who for some related reasons have no propensity for becoming authors. This implies that some living individuals, who have potential for writing, must shelter or adopt a number of potential authors within their biological individualities. What is pending to be actualized in the writing of one individual is the potentiality of many authors, i.e. those creative individuals who have no need or taste for living, in the same way as many living individuals have no need or taste for writing.

The deficiency of previous theories was to confuse these two aspects of writing, a biological individual and an authorial personality. Poststructuralist theory contributed to the solution of this question only negatively, by denying the attributes of a creative author to a biological individual. What logically follows is that we should also deny the attributes of a biological individual to a creative author. We have to split these naive equations of naturalistic fallacy. But we also have to proceed beyond the limits of this two-fold denial. Now the question has to be solved in a more constructive way, by positing hyper-authorship as the potential for an infinite self-differentiation of an (actual) individual as well as creative integration of different (virtual) individuals in the process of writing. The deconstruction of authorship opens way to the construction of hyper-authorship.

The basic principle of writing is the excess of signifiers over signifieds. Every single thing can be designated in many ways. This excess of signification generates synonyms, metaphors, paraphrases, parodies, parables, and other figurative and elliptical modes of writing. Furthermore, this principle applies to the overabundance of interpretations over the text which, again and again, becomes a single signified for proliferating critical discourses. What hasn't yet been discussed is the extension of this principle to the sphere of authorship. The excess of authorial personalities and their unlimited proliferation beyond the scope of an individual writing is the final surplus of the creative signification. The one who was believed to produce the excess now becomes the product of this excess. The respectable and indivisible Mr. Author gives way to the multiplicity of hyper-authors integrating and dividing their visions and efforts.

I believe that in the course of time hyper-authorship will become a conventional device not only in creative, but also in scholarly writing since it becomes impossible for a postmodern intellectual to adhere strictly to one position or one methodology in the matters of his/her profession. The need for the development of new, hypothetical methods of research (and which method is not hypothetical?) will bring about hyper-scholars who would pursue several alternative ways of argumentation mutually exclusive and complementary in the expanded universe of virtual knowledge.

When differences multiply and overlap with each other, we can detect a principally new phenomenon that can be called "interference." This means not only the act of interfering, but, to cite an encyclopedia, a specific "wave phenomenon that results from the mutual effect of two or more waves passing through a given region at the same time, producing reinforcement at some points and neutralization at other points." When hyper-authors pass together through a "given region" of creativity, their individualities are neutralizing and reinforcing each other at different points, the result being very expressive and contrastive picture of the world reminiscent of the patterns of a butterfly's wings colored, incidentally, by the same process of optical interference. Thus, difference progresses to the stage of interference, as the mature form of multidimensional integration-through-differentiation.

Let me share with you one secret. When you confided to me that it was not Yasusada but you who actually wrote his poems, I remained hesitant about the meaning of this statement, perceiving it as a possibility for still another round or level of interpretative play between these two possible authorships. What is essential here is not the difference between Motokiyu and Yasusada but their mutual interference. Finally, do we know, following the famous parable of Chuang Tzu, is it Chuang Tzu who sees a butterfly in his dream, or is it a butterfly who dreams of herself being Chuang Tzu? Are you absolutely sure that it's you who invented Yasusada, not the other way round?

Let's leave this divination to critics and literary historians, and let's proceed with the fact that both of these potential authorships are maintained on the level of "hyper", i.e., are mutually transferable without determination of the "origin" which is impossible, as you know, according to the theory of the trace. There is a trace of Yasusada in you, and there is a trace of Ivan Solovyov in me, but the origins of these traces are lost and irrecoverable, or even never existed. What is important to discuss is the relationship among these traces, not their relation to the "pseudo" origin. What becomes "pseudo" under this new mode of writing is not the name of the fictional author but the identity of the "original" author. Biologically and historically, I am Mikhail Epstein, but as an author, I am a complex relationship of several authorial personalities (some of them remain unknown even to myself), among whom Mikhail Epstein has no authorial privilege on the ground of the simple fact that he has some extra-textual body.

I also can imagine a journal (an annual?) inviting the contributions of transpersonal authors and elaborating the theory of hyper-authorship. The title might be TBA meaning "trans-biological authorship" and at the same time "To Be Announced," an abbreviation for something that has not yet and perhaps never will be determined.

I'm glad you found something new in *After the Future* and singled out "The Lyrical Museum"—this is one of my "favorites" among my own writings. I would be delighted if you could find a public outlet for your thoughts on "being in the world" and "sanctity of the unknown".

Cordially,

all of us, including Mikhail Epstein

NOTE:
*The materials on the Japanese poet Araki Yasusada (1907-1972), a survivor of Hiroshima, were published in *Grand Street, Conjunctions, Abiko Quarterly, First Intensity, Stand,* and *The American Poetry Review,* among a variety of other publications. Gradually the rumor began circulating that Araki Yasusada did not exist and that the poems were a "hoax" perpetrated by the contemporary Japanese-American author Tosa Motokiyu (who passed away Summer 1996) and/or by the executor of his will, the American poet Kent Johnson. See the discussion of this "hoax" issue and its ethical and aesthetical implications in *Lingua Franca* (November 1996) and *Countermeasures: A Magazine of Poetry and Ideas* , No.5. For more details on the "Yasusada case," see the section "Commentary and Hypotheses" below.

Mikhail Epstein

The work of Araki Yasusada has been appearing in numerous publications of late and has been provoking quite a bit of discussion in the world of poetry. I say "world" because poets and critics are not only avidly speculating about the work in the United States, but they are also beginning to do so in England, Australia, Japan, Russia, Italy, Spain, and Mexico, where selections and critical commentary have recently appeared. It is understandable why the Yasusada phenomenon has caused such fascination and controversy, for it is, without doubt, one of the most enigmatic and provocative authorial mysteries of 20th century poetry.

Originally presented in various journals as translations from the posthumously discovered notebooks of Yasusada, a purported survivor of the bombing of Hiroshima, the writing has recently been revealed by its "caretakers," Kent Johnson and Javier Alvarez (two individuals whose existence is empirically verifiable) as the creation of their former and now deceased roommate, Tosa Motokiyu, who has been credited in all previous publications as the main "translator" of Yasusada's work. Johnson and Alvarez assert that Tosa Motokiyu is the hypernym for an author whose actual identity they are under instructions to never reveal.

As the reader shall see, I came into contact with this work through two fortuitous occurrences, first in 1990 and then in 1995; but it was in January of 1996 that I became more intimate with it, when I received a letter and package of Yasusada materials from Motokiyu, who explained that he had been urged by "our mutual friend" Kent Johnson and his own interest in my recent book, *After the Future*, to write to me. In this letter he acknowledged to be the empirical writer of the Yasusada materials, and he asked for my thoughts on the implications inherent in such a scrambling of authorial identities. Indeed, I wrote him back a lengthy reply, only to learn from Kent Johnson this past summer that he had died not long after receiving my letter.

Like some other critics and scholars, I have reflected on the matter of Yasusada in these past months, and as I have done so, certain curious coincidences and parallel strands have emerged. Is it possible that my connection to this work has a more personal tie that I was not at first cognizant of? Is it possibly the case that the author whose hyper-identity is Tosa Motokiyu already knew of me many years ago, when we both were citizens of the bygone Soviet Union, and that his announced "death" is meant as a metaphor for his "death as an author"? I believe that the answer to these questions is very possibly "yes," and I write now to offer the following two hypotheses concerning the authorial origins of Yasusada. I do so not to try to to "solve" the matter (for paradoxes are not to be solved), but rather to suggest possible layers of hyper-authorship whose consideration may enrich the further interpretation and evaluation of this many-dimensioned work.

Before beginning, I think it is worth pointing out that Emily Nussbaum's discussion (Nov/Dec,96) in *Lingua Franca* regarding the presence of Yasusada poems in Kent Johnson's doctoral dissertation does in no way settle the question of the Yasusada authorship. In fact, as I believe my remarks will suggest, it is quite feasible that Johnson placed this work in his dissertation at the request of its actual author. Such a gesture would have been perfectly consistent, for example, with the "conceptualist" aesthetic of one of the writers I discuss below. I might further say, in regards to this matter, that I happened to be a guest lecturer in Bowling Green, Ohio, in the spring of 1990, and was invited to attend Johnson's dissertation defense, which fell by strange coincidence, on the day of my arrival there. As he began, in front of a table full of solemn professors, to speak about the poems of Yasusada, two other graduate students seated on the floor behind him began (carefully following notations set down in copies of Johnson's lecture) to loudly exclaim certain utterances in English and Russian, and to blow, strike, and drum on an array of Asian musical instruments. This they did for the next fifteen minutes or so, while Johnson presented a collage of theoretical and poetic propositions. Although the professors on Johnson's committee seemed very perplexed, I can attest that this was truly a strange and memorable event, one very similar in flavor to a conceptualist poetry evening in my native Moscow.

This parallel was all the more vivid to me because my lecture at Bowling Green and the subsequent conversation with Kent Johnson and his colleagues was devoted in a significant part to conceptualism and the construction of multiple authorships. Of this conversation published later, I will cite only one passage that relates directly to the current discussion on the authorship of Yasusada's poetry: "After deconstruction comes an epoch of pure constructivism. Anything can be constructed now. As one of my philosophical characters says—most of my recent works are constituted not by my own thoughts, but by those of my characters—a word cannot be exact, cannot be precise, so it must be brave. Deconstruction demonstrated that a word can't be precise, it can't designate any particular thing. But what remains to be done with the word? To be brave, to use it in all senses that are possible to it. This [is] the new domain of construction which comes after . . . deconstruction."[1]

Included into this domain is, first of all, the construction of authorship, as implied in those philosophical characters in my own work about whom and on whose behalf I am speaking. This explains why I became so intrigued by the phenomenon of Yasusada and now attempt to look into the enigma of his origin. Now it depends on the readers to decide if the following hypotheses pursue the goal of deconstruction of Yasusada or rather can serve as an example of critical constructionism.

Hypothesis #1: The Yasusada manuscript, *Doubled Flowering: From The Notebooks Of Araki Yasusada*, was originally composed in Russian by the famous writer Andrei Bitov and then translated by Kent Johnson and at least one Russian-speaking informant into English. I'll try to substantiate this version with irrefutable facts.

Bitov, born 1937, is Russia's major contemporary novelist, the principal representative of, and, to a certain degree, the founder of Russian postmodernism. His work generated a number of famous hyper-authors, among them Lev Odoevtsev, a literary scholar and the protagonist of Bitov's major novel *Pushkin's House*, and Urbino Vanoski, a writer of mixed Polish, Italian and Japanese origin, the hyper-author of another of Bitov's novels, *A Professor of Symmetry*, which is annotated as "a translation from English without a dictionary."

I have been maintaining friendly ties with Bitov since the late 1960s and have first-hand information about the following. In the mid-1960s Bitov—by that time already one of the leading figures of the so-called "youth prose"—received an invitation to visit Japan through the official channels of the Soviet Writers' Union. However, he was denied an exit visa by Soviet authorities, who claimed that he was too ideologically immature for such a responsible trip to a capitalist country (he was suspected to be a hidden dissident, almost rightfully, as presumably 80% of the Soviet intelligentsia were at that time). One can easily imagine both the excitement and disappointment of a young writer who spent two or three subsequent years reapplying for this trip and reassuring the authorities of his "maturity" in vain. This bitter experience inspired him to write a novel *Iaponiia* (*Japan*), about the country he never saw but tried to reinvent in his imagination. Two planes alternated in this novel: the bureaucratic trials of a young author haunting the thresholds of high Soviet authorities, and imaginary landscapes and poetic visions of Japan, including fragments of an imaginary anthology of contemporary Japanese poetry. Incidentally, though Bitov never considered himself a real poet, he has hyper-authored several brilliant poems allegedly written by some of his characters (in particular, Aleksei Monakhov, the protagonist of Bitov's "dotted" novel *The Days Of A Man*). I assume that Bitov's novel *Iaponiia* (whose other working title was actually "Dreams about Japan") was a kind of symmetrical response to the 18th century Japanese masterpiece *Dreams about Russia*, written by Kodayu Daikokuya, a treatise which mixes pseudo-ethnographic description with lyrical visionary passages. This book was twice translated into Russian, and I have no doubts Bitov was intimate with it.

With the coming of glasnost', Bitov intended to publish his novel

Iaponiia after some additional stylistic elaboration. I was very intrigued by this plot, especially after *A Professor of Symmetry* came out, with a brilliant stylization of a contemporary multi-ethnic Western author, slightly in Conrad's or Nabokov's vein (English was not hyper-author Vanoski's native language; hence Bitov's translation from English into Russian of a novel which itself was presumably translated from his mother language into English, at least in the bilingual imagination of the imagined author). I expected that Bitov's *Iaponiia* would again induce a case of "doubled authorship," now with a Japanese hyper-author. According to Bitov's account, *Iaponiia* was almost finished. But gradually all rumors about its pending publication disappeared, and my direct questions addressed to Bitov failed to receive any definite answer. Bitov complained that he was burdened with numerous urgent literary projects and administrative responsibilities. Indeed, since the early 1990's he has been the president of Russian Pen-Club. Thus, the publication of *Iaponiia*, with a poetic anthology as its supplement, was postponed for an indefinite period.

The last time I saw Bitov was December 11, 1995 when he visited Emory by my invitation to give a lecture on Russian postmodernism. In our conversation he confirmed again, with a visible reluctance, that *Iaponiia* will be published in due time, but probably "in a modified form" (he did not go into details). On December 29 of the same year, in downtown Chicago, at the annual convention of the Modern Language Association, I met by chance Kent Johnson, whom I had not seen for several years. He shared with me news on the rising posthumous star of Araki Yasusada, and gave me some copies of Yasusada's publications. Not immediately, but with an increasing feeling of right guess, I recognized Bitov's stylistic charm in these English verses allegedly translated from Japanese... But why not directly from Russian?

The point is that Kent Johnson (as the compiler and editor of a well-known and critically acclaimed anthology of contemporary Russian verse, *Third Wave: The New Russian Poetry*)[2] had much more grounded and first-hand familiarity with Russian poetry than with Japanese. The question that is raised is this: Is it possible that there is a connection between Kent Johnson, who is now prominently connected to Yasusada's legacy, and Andrei Bitov, a master of hyperauthorship and the author of the still unpublished novel *Iaponiia*? Let me further explain.

I first met Kent Johnson in St. Petersburg (then Leningrad, the native city, incidentally, of Bitov) in 1989, at a conference on contemporary Russian culture. Kent was then busy collecting materials for his English anthology of the newest trends in Russian poetry of 1970s-80s. This anthology came out with my afterword, from University of Michigan Press in 1992 and had a significant success, particularly in the world of Slavic literature: it was the first book in English representing the "new wave" of Russian poetry, and, most valuably, it contained, in addition to verses, theoretical manifestoes of the poets. Kent Johnson and his co-editor, Steven Ashby, managed to make a superb choice of authors and their representative works, as well as of skillful translators, for this unique collection. This project by itself would have justified Kent's trip to St. Petersburg, but, as I suspect is possible now, it was in Russia that he got the impetus for the preparation of another anthology, this time a Japanese one, subsumed under the name of a central hyper-author (Yasusada), but including two of Yasusada's renga collaborators, Ozaki Kusatao and Akutagawa Fusei, and their three contemporary translators, Tosa Motokiyu, Okura Kyojin, and Ojiu Norinaga. I am amazed with what subtle skills this anthology has been translated from Russian into English in order to be finally presented as originally Japanese. Now I can also understand why Bitov withdrew his intention to publish *Iaponiia* under his own name. To become a part of a foreign culture is a more inspiring, generous, and at the same time ambitious enterprise than just to add still another piece to the treasury of one's native language.

Yasusada's work is conceived not just as a poetical collection, but as a novel with its own sub-plot (the editorial piecing together of the fragmented record of a Hiroshima survivor), cast in the multi-generic form of diaries, letters, verses, comments, etc. The meta-genre of "novel in verses" is deeply rooted in Russian literary tradition, with Pushkin's *Eugene Onegin* as its prototype—the major source of Bitov's inspiration throughout all his creative search and especially in his major novel *Pushkin's House*. No wonder that the novel *Iaponiia* proved to be not just a novel with "poetic supplement" as was intended initially, but "a novel in verses," or, more precisely, "a novel with verses." Every reader of Yasusada's texts will agree that verses constitute only one aspect of its larger literary whole which, like both Pushkin's and Bitov's novels, include numerous self-commenting pages, lyrical digressions, and critical reflections... This is truly a poetic novel of Yasusada's life, a novel in the traditions of Russian literature which now, with the aid of Kent Johnson's mediation, again invests its inspirations into the treasury of Japanese literature, but now even in the more palpable and congenial form of "a newly discovered author."

In Russian literature, authors like Pushkin, Dostoevsky, Tolstoy and Chekhov, were for a long time the moral and artistic authorities for Japanese literature; now, with Bitov-Johnson's contribution, Russian literature becomes an indispensable part of Japanese literature, of its novelistic flesh and poetic blood. As a scholar of Russian literature, I can only rejoice at the fact of this transcultural interaction and the resulting synthesis.

Hypothesis #2: This, I believe, is the least hypothetical of the two, being merely a combined statement of several well known facts. Among Russian authors presented in Kent Johnson's anthology of contemporary Russian poetry, one of the most preeminent figures is Dmitry Prigov, a close acquaintance of Bitov, and a central proponent of Russian Conceptualism, who is known for his poems and whole collections written on behalf of various characters and mentalities belonging to different cultures. As Prigov puts it in his manifesto published in Johnson's anthology, "the heroes of my poems have become different linguistic layers . . . A shimmering relationship between the author and the text has developed, in which it is very hard to define (not only for the reader but for the author, too) the degree of sincerity in the immersion in the text and the purity and distance of the withdrawal from it. . . . The result is some kind of quasi-lyrical poems written by me under a feminine name, when I am of course not concerned with mystification but only show the sign of the lyrical poem's position, which is mainly associated with feminine poetry"[3]

In 1987 or 1988 Prigov circulated a collection of verses on behalf of a Chinese she-poet, thus helping to fill the gap of female authorship in the highly developed but almost exclusively male-oriented Chinese classic tradition. Further, he planned to expand the cultural geography of his hyperauthorship by introducing a collection by a Japanese poet with "a rather unusual but universally comprehensible fate and sensibility." This collection was never published under the name of Prigov himself, and I submit that in this case the project of hyperauthorship underwent a further mysterious expansion to acquire an international set of hyper-authors, hypereditors, etc., along the lines of a global poetic plot (imitating and parodying the 'Zionist-masonic conspiracy as exposed in "The Protocols of Zion"). Prigov once, in the spirit of 'new sincerity', confessed to me his "masonic" conspiracy for the triumph of creative impersonality throughout the world of art.

Precisely by the time Prigov's Japanese collection was due to be finished (1989), Kent Johnson came for his first and only visit to Leningrad to meet with Prigov and other poets participating in the future Russian anthology. From my continuous personal talks with Prigov at this time (we even spent a rather "sincere" night of discussions and confessions in the apartment of our common friend poet Viktor Krivulin) I could conclude that along with the poems he passed to Kent for this anthology, there was an additional set of materials large enough to form a separate collection which, it is easy to conclude, came to be known as "Doubled Flowering" by Araki Yasusada.

I want to underscore once more that everything aforesaid is only a hypothesis, though all mentioned facts are true. I daresay this kind of hypothesis does not need a further factual verification, inasmuch as the true identity of the person named Tosa Motokiyu (who, as I mentioned earlier, is now claimed by Johnson and Alvarez to be the "real" author of the work) is never to be revealed, according to his own last will. A question poses itself: Whose will is this, if its author refuses to be attributed its authorship? This is the same type of paradox that we find in the most famous of logical paradoxes of "liar's type": "The liar says that he is always lying. Is it a truth or a lie?" If we believe Motokiyu's testament (that is, his statement that his true name is not to be revealed) then this is not Motokiyu's testament.

A vicious circle? But is not the same circle inscribed into another declaration of authorship? Is Shakespeare Shakespeare? Let us suggest that whoever Shakespeare was he succeeded to produce, in addition to *Hamlet* and other classical plays, the most enigmatic of his creations—the author named "Shakespeare," the one who wrote both prophetic *Hamlet* and his own almost illiterate will.

The vicious circle is a creative one. An author's imperative: to create an author. How can we trust a doctor who is permanently sick? There is a biblical saying: "Physician, heal thyself." How can we trust an author who limits himself to inferior characters, like tsars, generals, business people, etc., and cannot create an Author?

Thus we should be grateful to Motokiyu, who succeeded to create Yasusada and, even more, his friends, translators, editors, and executors. But who created Motokiyu? And who created his creator? The answer is infinitely deferred, to use the deconstructionist cliche, but what is more important and goes beyond the realm of deconstruction is the construction of infinite authors in the place of the absent single one. By this I do not mean to imply that the questioning of and quest for an original authorship should be qualified as a critical fallacy; the point, rather, is that the dispersion of creative origins is an artistic provocation that brings forth the possibilities of infinite answers. Why shouldn't such provocation productively exist alongside genetic paradigms of authorship? Is not the goal of creativity the excess of meanings over signs, and, therefore, the excess of authors over texts, since each additional authorship is a way to change radically the overall meaning of the text? Each text is allowed to have as many authors as it needs to have in order to become infinitely meaningful.

Vladimir Nabokov once remarked on what makes literature different from the "true story" or "the poetry of testimony": "Literature was born not the day when a boy crying 'wolf, wolf' came running out of the Neanderthal valley with a big gray wolf at his heels: literature was born on the day when a boy came crying 'wolf, wolf' and there was no wolf behind him."[4]

A friend of mine, with whom I shared this observation, remarked pessimistically: "In our wretched times, when the boy runs in crying 'wolf, wolf' no poetry is born whatsoever — he will simply be dragged to court for making 'false statements' and 'disturbing the peace' of the pedestrian-minded." Some will regard such a view as overly gloomy, but it does suggest why, in our times, the boy might do well to disappear together with the ghostly wolf he dared to so bravely herald. In other words, the author is drawn to become fictitious in the way fiction is itself; the author shares the destiny of her characters and becomes one of them, like a chameleon—an illusion among illusions. Perhaps a new kind of literature is being given birth these days—one where neither the wolf nor the boy

145

is to be found, even though the heart-rending cries go on echoing in the villagers' ears.

But wait, object the villagers, for in the meantime rumors about the wolf and the boy who supposedly are "never present" become more insistent and repetitious. Isn't this play of language with no ground exactly what we know as postmodernism? If the wolf in your little parable represents the objective truth of classical art, while the boy represents the subjectivist pathos of modernism, what, then, is the truth and the pathos enacted by their vanishing? Is it not a blasphemy to "post-modernize" such a deeply pathetic experience as conveyed by Yasusada's poetry? If everything becomes fiction, including the author, what is left that is real?

Theodor Adorno, with even deeper pessimism than my friend above, famously proclaimed that there can be no poetry after Auschwitz. We might likewise conclude that there can be no poetry after Hiroshima. But is this true? Could it be, instead, that poetry, as humanity on the whole, must become wholly different from what it used to be in order to fulfill its human calling after Hiroshima? If so, then the work of Yasusada can be seen as pointing toward one possible form of renewal. For in it, poetry reaches beyond the individual's original self-expression, beyond the "flowering" of one person, to become something other: a shared imagining and expression of humanity—of Russians, Japanese, Americans, of any nationality. Yasusada's fragments, letters, and poems become, through the egoless generosity of a person or persons we call Motokiyu, an appeal for a transpersonal (and thus selfless and in a sense authorless) empathy. Perhaps we can say this: In Yasusada there exist as many potential authorships as there are individuals in the world who are aware of Hiroshima and associate themselves with the fate of its victims and survivors.

In conclusion, I must state again that all facts cited in this letter concerning real names, persons and historical circumstances, are true. It is only the interpretation of these facts which can claim the higher status of a hypothesis.

POSTSCRIPTUM

On November 15, 1996, my way crossed with Andrei Bitov's at a Slavic conference in Boston. I told him very briefly about Yasusada and shared with him my hypothesis about his potential authorship. He thought for a while and then noted: "The more hypothetical is one's approach to an author, the more truthful it may finally prove to be." "Does this relate to this specific case?" I asked directly. He evaded the direct answer and continued: "The value of hypothesis is to predict a thing which cannot be observed. The value of an authorship is to make possible what is impossible. A critical hypothesis about an author is just a reversed projection of his own creativity and does not need any further justification. As you know, some of my characters are literary scholars, which presumes that some literary scholars . . ." At this moment—we were strolling around the book exhibition—an acquaintance of Bitov approached him and distracted us from the conversation. Unfortunately, later on this day we had no opportunity to talk privately, and neither of us wanted to bring this topic to public attention. Two details of this short exchange need to be emphasized. 1)Bitov didn't ask me what Yasusada's works were about. 2) Anyone familiar with Yasusada's style cannot but recognize its echoes in Bitov's manner of coining paradoxes.

NOTES

1. Ellen E. Berry, Kent Johnson, Anesa Miller-Pogacar, "Postcommunist Postmodernism: An interview with Mikhail Epstein, *Common Knowledge*, Oxford University Press, 1993, Vol.2, No.3, p.110.
2. *Third Wave: The New Russian Poetry*, ed. Kent Johnson and Stephen M. Ashby. Ann Arbor: The University of Michigan Press, 1992
3. *Third Wave: The New Russian Poetry*, ibid., p. 102.
4. *The Writer's Quotation Book: A Literary Companion*, ed. James Chariton, New York: Penguin, 1986, p. 9.

In Search of the Authentic Other:
The Poetry of Araki Yasusada

Marjorie Perloff

I

The July/August 1996 issue of *American Poetry Review* featured a special supplement called "Doubled Flowering: From the Notebooks of Araki Yasusada." Translations of this Japanese poet had already appeared in such leading periodicals as *Grand Street, Conjunctions, Aerial, First Intensity*, and Jon Silkin's British poetry journal *Stand*. According to Yasusada's three translators—Tosa Motokiyu, Okura Kyojin, and Ojiu Norinaga—all three, like the poet, from Hiroshima—Yasusada's notebooks were discovered by his son in 1980, eight years following the poet's death. These fourteen notebooks contained dozens of poems, drafts, English class assignments, diary entries, drawings, letters, and recordings of Zen dokusan encounters. None of this material, it seems, had been published during Yasusada's lifetime. The following biographical note, prepared by the translators, appears, with slight variation in each of the periodicals cited above:

> Yasusada was born in 1907 in the city of Kyoto, where he lived until 1921, when his family moved to Hiroshima. He attended Hiroshima University sporadically between 1925 and 1928, with the intent of receiving a degree in Western Literature. Due, however, to his father's illness, he was forced, in the interests of the family, to undertake full-time employment with the postal service and withdraw from his formal studies.
>
> In 1930 he married his only wife Nomura, with whom he had two daughters and a son. In 1936, Yasusada was conscripted into the Japanese Imperial Army and worked as a clerk in the Hiroshima division of the Military Postal Service. His wife and youngest daughter Chieko, died instantly in the atomic blast on August 6. His daughter Akiko survived, yet perished less than four years later from radiation sickness. His son, Yasunari, an infant at the time, was with relatives outside the city.
>
> Yasusada died in 1972 after a long struggle with cancer.[1]

We are further told that Yasusada was active in avant-garde groups of the pre-War period like *Soun* [*Layered Clouds*] and the experimental renga circle *Kai* [*Oars*] and that in the sixties he "discovered" Jack Spicer and Roland Barthes (APR 23). A 1967 letter to his renga collaborator Akutagawa Fusei, included in the *APR* selection, talks enthusiastically of

Barthes's *Empire of Signs* (24), and the translators further comment that there are undated haiku that "unmistakably bear the stamp of the famous poet, and Holocaust survivor, Paul Celan," whose work "was read by the Layered Clouds group and critically discussed by them" (26).

The poems—of which more in a moment—have aroused great interest and enthusiasm. In response to the *Conjunctions* portfolio, the poet Ron Silliman told his friends and fellow poets on the Buffalo Poetics List that the journal had introduced "a poet whose work simply takes my breath away." Citing the short "Telescope with Urn," which begins with the line "The image of the galaxies spreads out like a cloud of sperm,"[2] Silliman remarks, "There's an elevation of tone in these poems that reminds me more of Michael Palmer than Spicer, perhaps because the translators are all Hiroshima poets (one of whom seems to spend half of each year in Sebastapol [CA], although I don't know if he's known to [David] Bromige or to Cydney Chadwick). These works kept me up last night and probably will again for another night or three. I recommend them highly."[3]

Yet even as the Yasusada poems were prompting this sort of response, the word was leaking out that there was no Yasusada, that indeed the whole Yasusada publication was an elaborate hoax, perpetrated, most probably, by one Kent Johnson, a young poet-professor at Highland Community College in Freeport, Illinois. Johnson, the co-editor, with Stephen M. Ashby, of an anthology of New Russian poetry called *The Third Wave* (Ann Arbor: University of Michigan Press, 1992), and, with Craig Paulenich, of an anthology of contemporary American Buddhist poetry called *Beneath a Single Moon* (Boston and London: Shambhala, 1991), still doesn't admit to inventing Yasusada; he now declares that the "real" author is the Yasusada translator, Tosa Motokiyu (a pseudonym, in its turn, of yet another unknown poet who is safely dead). But when *American Poetry Review* and *Stand* recently demanded the return of their author's payment, it was to Kent Johnson they addressed their letters. And since he is at the very least the middleman and facilitator of the "hoax," as a matter of convenience, I shall refer to him here as its author.

According to *Lingua Franca*, which ran an article on "The Hiroshima Poetry Hoax" in its November 1996 issue, Arthur Vogelsang, one of the three editors of *American Poetry Review*, went so far as to call Johnson's deception a "criminal act."[4] Wesleyan University Press, which had contemplated publishing a volume of Yasusada poems, immediately dropped the project: an anonymous reader, whose report was made available to me by Kent Johnson, expressed great admiration for the poems but felt queasy at the suggestion that the manuscript might be a hoax, it being out of bounds, in the reader's estimation, for anyone to impersonate a figure as *ipso facto* tragic as a Hiroshima survivor.

While these editors and publishers have taken issue with what they perceive as the immorality of the hoax, scholars have objected to its inaccuracy. "This is just Japanized crap," John Solt, a professor of Japanese culture at Amherst College, told *Lingua Franca*'s Emily Nussbaum. "It plays into the American idea of what is interesting about Japanese culture—Zen, haiku, anything seen as exotic—and gets it all wrong, adding Western humor and irony" (LF 83). Yet this estimate may also be a simplification. For Solt, like APR's Vogelsang and the anonymous reader for Wesleyan, are assuming that Kent Johnson (or whoever the "real" Yasusada turns out to be) produced as accurate a simulation as possible, whereas the fact is that the author has put in, surely not unintentionally, any number of clues that raise questions as to Yasusada's authenticity. Consider the following:

1) The name Araki Yasusada means, in Japanese usage, that Araki is the family name, Yasusada the first name. Araki is indeed a common family name in Japanese.[5] Yet the "translators" regularly refer to the poet as Yasusada, which would be equivalent to referring to Roland Barthes as Roland. By the same token, the poet's wife's name, Nomura, is in fact a family name, not a first name, so the reference given would be like Robert Lowell referring to his wife as Hardwick. Again, "Motokiyu" is a misspelling for "Motokiyo" and "Ojiu" should be "Ogyu." So the author is, at the very least, playing fast and loose with Japanese names.

2) It is hard to accept the explanation that Yasusada, who was supposedly active in avant-garde groups in the 1920s and 30s, never tried to publish any of his postwar poems and that they were entirely unknown in his native Japan, where he seems to have had the liveliest of correspondences with his fellow poets.

3) Yasusada, we are told, "attended Hiroshima University sporadically between 1925 and 1928, with the intent of receiving a degree in Western Literature." His attendance must have been sporadic indeed since Hiroshima University was not founded until 1949. As for studying Western Literature, there would have been no such subject. English Literature, French Literature—these were and are academic subjects, but the idea of Yasusada studying "Western" literature looks like an American representation of what a Japanese might do.

4) Yasusada ostensibly came under the influence of Jack Spicer in the mid-60s, which is to say when Yasusada was in his late fifties. This is implausible on a number of counts. First, Jack Spicer was an unknown coterie poet at the time; indeed, he is still largely an unknown coterie poet, whose work does not appear in any of the major anthologies. It is, of course, conceivable that the poet's friend Natsume Kuribayashi brought the book *After Lorca* (1957) back to Hiroshima from a visit to San Francisco. But if so, Yasusada must have been the only poet in Japan who took an interest in Spicer.

5) Roland Barthes is listed as a second major influence. But *The Empire of Signs*, which Yasusada supposedly pored over in 1967, wasn't even published in French until 1970. The U.S. edition dates from 1982. There is thus no way Yasusada could have read this book, and Barthes' earlier works were, like Spicer's, only very little known outside France.

6) Paul Celan, ostensibly read and studied by the *Soun* group before World War II, did not start publishing—and then in German—until 1952. So the notion that he was closely studied in the Japan of the thirties is totally absurd.

7) Finally, there is a wonderful clinamen in the November 7, 1967 letter to the poet's collaborator, Fusei. "Besides Spicer," writes Yasusada, "there are interesting new books here waiting for you by poets named Gary Snyder, Bob Kaufman, Kenneth Rexroth, Howard McCord, Robert Creeley, Helen Adams [*sic*], and Lawrence Ferlinghetti. Kuribayashi tells me that they were strongly recommended to him by McCord, the owner of City Lights Bookstore, a popular bookseller in San Francisco." (APR 26). Now we can, with a stretch of the imagination, accept the fact that the sixty-year old Hiroshima survivor, whose poetic habits would most probably have been formed much earlier, would interest himself in the newest Beat poets from the U.S. But the give-away in the list is Howard McCord, not a Bay Area poet at all but a poet-professor from Bowling Green University who was Kent Johnson's college mentor. Hence the sly footnote provided by Yasusada's translators: "Yasusada is confused here, as the real owner of the City Lights Bookstore is Lawrence Ferlinghetti" (APR 26).

Clearly, if the inventor of the Yasusada persona had wanted to cover his tracks, he need never have mentioned Howard McCord or the influence of Celan on Yasusada, much less the Japanese poet's reading of Barthes's *Empire of Signs*. We can only conclude that the "real" author wanted his readers to find something perplexing in the Yasusada archive, that he purposely set the stage for suspicion. The very first poem in the APR Supplement, for example, is represented as a "modest gathering of haiku" sent to Yasusada's friend, the haiku master Ogiwara Seisensui.[6] The poem is dated March 30, 1925 and goes like this:

> iris moon sheaths
> scubadivers chrysanthemums also
> deer inlets dream
> oars   this earth
> geese lined bowl
> shard   so horizon
> cod dried dawn
> bones sky written
> lichened space rock
> fossils celebrating investors
> crematorium shared persimmon
> hyacinth clustered strangers
> cranes three words (APR 24)

This looks rather like a page of ideogram transcriptions from the Ernest Fenollosa notebooks that Ezra Pound used when composing his *Cathay*:

gathering gathering fixed clouds
pattering pattering temporary rain
eight surface same dark
flat road this wide & flat[7]

But what are those "scubadivers" doing between the chrysanthemums and the iris? The technology of scuba diving was not invented until World War II, which also gave Yasusada the currency of the word "crematorium." As for "investors" in line 10, this reference to capitalist activity does not exactly belong to the haiku discourse radius of hyacinths and persimmons, cranes and lichen. The perspective is rather like Pound's in the *Homage to Sextus Propertius* (1917), where the lines "My cellar does not date from Numa Pompilius, / Nor bristle with wine jars," is followed by the startling, "Nor is it equipped with a frigidaire patent."[8] What such overlays do is to take the material in question out of its temporal and spatial frame, problematizing its representation and tone. And this, for Johnson-Yasusada, as for Pound-Propertius, is clearly intentional.

Why, then, given such obvious clues as "scubadivers" and "crematorium," have editors and readers so quickly assumed that they are dealing with an "authentic" Hiroshima poet? We cannot just dismiss these disseminators as ignorant, for they include editors and writers as varied as they are talented. Bradford Morrow, for one, came to *Conjunctions* as an Ezra Pound scholar and editor; he published, for example, the excellent facsimile editions of the Pound-Wyndham Lewis Vorticist magazine *Blast*. Rod Smith's *Aerial* has played a central role in the introduction of radical new poetries: the issue that includes Yasusada's works also contains a preview of Joan Retallack's *Musicage* as well as Cage's own piece "Art Is Either A Complaint Or Do Something Else" and some of Jackson Mac Low's *Merzgedichte in Memoriam Kurt Schwitters*.[9] And there are few contemporary poets more widely read, engaged, and intellectually lively than the poet-editor-critic Ron Silliman, who declared that Yasusada's memorable phrases kept him awake at night.

II

To understand why Silliman and Morrow, Jean Stein of *Grand Street*, and Jon Silkin, the longtime editor of the British radical quarterly *Stand* were "taken in" by the Yasusada manuscripts, we must look at the larger issues of multicultural and cross-cultural reception on the current poetry scene. The Yasusada case, I shall argue here, can be understood as a reaction formation experienced by a literary community that no longer trusts the individual talent to rise above mass culture and hence must find a poetry worthy of its attention in increasingly remote and improbable locations. "Excellence," now largely dismissed as an essentialist concept, is subordinated to issues of agency and positionality, the master text here no doubt still being Michel Foucault's famous 1969 essay, "What Is an Author?"

Foucault's central position, which has come to be *de rigueur* in the academy, is that it is the culture that constructs or *writes* the author, not vice-versa: "the essential basis of . . . writing is not the exalted emotions related to the act of composition or the insertion of a subject into language. Rather, it is primarily concerned with creating an opening where the writing subject endlessly disappears."[10] Disappears because, far from being "free" to write whatever he or she wishes, the writing subject can only work within the limits of the dominant discourse and hence is no more than a function of the discourse within which it circulates. No longer then do we ask "What has [the author] revealed of his most profound self in his language"? The question is rather, "Where does [this discourse] come from; how is it circulated; who controls it? What placements are determined for possible subjects?" (MF 138). Who, in other words, is empowered to speak and from what position? And, once these questions become central, emphasis falls on those who have, thus far, not been empowered to speak— in earlier centuries, women and lower-class writers; in our own moment, the victims of oppression of whatever stamp: Colonialist, racist, sexist, homophobic, and so on.

In practice, of course, these questions of positionality and empowerment have become very complicated. In the case of Yasusada, it would be a simplification to suggest that the editors and readers who responded so warmly to the work did so only—or even primarily—because the poet was that rare thing, a previously unknown Hiroshima survivor, a witness to the events of August 6, 1945. But certainly the Hiroshima witnessing is a central factor in the equation. Let me explain.

From the fifties to the late eighties when the Cold War came to an end, and with it, the urgency of world-wide protests against the production and testing of nuclear weapons, an appreciable number of Japanese poetry books and anthologies appeared on the horrors of Hiroshima and Nagasaki. A recent such anthology is Jiro Nakano's *Outcry from the Inferno: Atom Bomb Tanka Anthology*.[11] The preface is by the leading tanka poet Seishi Toyota, a Hiroshima survivor who suffered from radiation poisoning and declared that "writing and reading atomic bomb tanka are my karma and life-long work" (p. xiii). The typical tanka in the anthology goes like this:

> Like a demon or ghost
> a man runs away
> staggering—
> with both hands
> hung loosely in front of him. (Ayako Etsuchi, OI 2)

or,

> A crowd of ten thousand
> are standing in despair
> with skins hanging

from red sores—
the scorched land of Hiroshima. (Hatsuko Miyamae, OI 51)
Or, occasionally more polemically:
Mothers, wives, sisters
and grandmothers—
remember your losses,
Stand up and fill those prisons.
Defy the draft! (Momoyo Ishii, OI 18)

These tanka are obviously more notable for their subject matter than for their poetic quality. A more sophisticated version of Japanese atomic bomb literature is found in Richard Minear's *Hiroshima: Three Witnesses*.[12] Minear's three are the fabulist Hara Tamiki, the novelist Ota Yoko, and the poet Toge Sankichi. Toge is probably the key figure in Hiroshima literature: his *Poems of the Atomic Bomb*, written in 1951 when he was already dying from a radiation-related illness, has gone through more than forty printings. Instead of the haiku and tanka he had used in his pre-war poetry, Toge here uses free verse, with much rhetorical variation: onomatopoeia, repetition, elaborate sound play. Here is the opening of "Dying" (in Minear's translation), a poem that Jerome Rothenberg and Pierre Joris have chosen for inclusion in the second volume of their *Poems for the Millennium*:

Loud in my ear: screams.
Soundlessly welling up,
pouncing on me:
space, all upside-down
Hanging, fluttering clouds of dust
smelling of smoke,
and, running madly about, figures.
"Ah,
get out
of here!"
Scattering fragments of brick,
I spring to my feet;
my body's
on fire. . . . (HTW 308)

And the poem concludes with a passage in which extinction is represented not only verbally but metrically, four one-word lines culminating in the silence of the final line, which contains no more than a single question mark:

Why here
by the side of the road

154

cut off, dear, from you;
why
must
I
die
? (HTW 310)

Toge is probably the most noted realist chronicler of the Hiroshima
tragedy: over and over again, he records the chaos and suffering of ordi-
nary people in the fire storms of August. A short poem of his called "Give
the People Back" appeared in a 1985 *American Poetry Review* portfolio on
Hiroshima poets, in which Suneko Yoshikawa presents four poems (one of
them her own), translated by the Canadian poet Steven Forth. Here a full
page of background information is followed by two short pages of poetry.
These poems are again straightforward and often polemic monologues, as
in the case of Hara Tamiki's "Water Please," with its lines like "Help me
help me / Water / Water/ Somewhere / Someone."[13]

But although the testimonials of the *hibakusha* (atomic bomb survivors)
continue to play a central role in Japanese culture, and although there has
been a definite market for Hiroshima-witness poems, especially in the
West, the fact is—and this will shed light on Yasusada's position—that
contemporary Japanese poets have been reluctant to write about
Hiroshima or, for that matter, about the culture of nuclear weapons. No
doubt, memories of a war that the then wholly nationalist, autocratic, and
bellicose Imperial Japanese government had initiated are too painful; for
those born after 1945, moreover, these memories no longer seem directly
relevant. "It is difficult," the young poet-scholar Nagahata Akitoshi
remarked in a letter to me (January 15, 1997), "for us to talk about
Hiroshima / Nagasaki, because to do so would always make us question
our subjectivity. We are sons and daughters of the people who were
bombed, but at the same time of the oppressors. We could blame our fate
on the politicians at the time (i.e., militarists) or on the war in the abstract.
But I think this is an evasion."

Nagahata's observations are confirmed by the literature. Open any vol-
ume like Leith Morton's *Anthology of Contemporary Japanese Poetry*[14] and
you will find an extraordinarily colloquial, often casual, postmodern poet-
ry that deals with every aspect of sexuality, with themes of longing and
frustration, memories of childhood, contemplation of urban congestion
and natural beauty, with self-interrogation and remorse, the relation of
private to public, individual identity to culture and to the natural world—
in short, pretty much all the themes that would characterize our own poet-
ry. Six of the sixteen poets in Morton's anthology are women—and very
emancipated women at that. The performance poet Shiraishi Kazuko (b.
1931), for example, has a poem written for her friend Sumiko's birthday
that is called "Penis" (*Dankon*) and begins:

God is not here but he exists
Also he is funny so
He's like a certain type of person

This time
Bringing a gigantic penis above
The horizon of my dream
He came for a picnic
By the way
I'm sorry
I didn't give anything to Sumiko for her birthday
The seed of the penis that God brought if only that
I want to send into
The delicate small sweet voice of
Sumiko on the end of the line (LM 197)

Shiraishi had worked closely with Kenneth Rexroth: her mode is a rib-ald version of Beat or San Francisco Renaissance poems, going back, per-haps, to the bitter-sweet erotic free verse poems of Apollinaire. Often, the poet's tone is one of detached bemusement, a tone we find most fully developed in the work of the celebrated postwar poet Tanikawa Shuntaro who has a predilection for short riddling lyrics or fables like "The Poet":

If there is a mirror the poet will always look into it
He makes certain whether or not he is a poet
Even if he reads poetry he doesn't know whether or not he's a poet
He firmly believes that if he looks at his face he can tell with a single
    glance
The poet is dreaming that one day
His face will be put on a stamp
He says he wants if possible to have his face on a really cheap stamp
Then he can have lots of people lick him
While his wife is frying some noodles
She has a sour puss (LM 358).

Tanikawa, Shiraishi—these are hardly well-known poets in the U.S. Indeed, the very *American Poetry Review* that published Yasusada and then called the submission of the manuscript a "criminal act," has, in the past fifteen years, published no other translations of contemporary Japanese poetry with the exception of the Hiroshima portfolio I cited above. Bengali women poets, underground Chinese, Polish and Rumanian, Nicaraguan, and South African poets—all these appear in the pages of APR as does a feature on two medieval Japanese women court poets, as translated by Jane Hirschfield and Mariko Aratani, and a special supplement on the Zen Master Muso (Muso Sosei,1275-1351) translated by W. S. Merwin with the

156

help of Soiku Shigematsu. But the new Japanese poets, whose brilliance and variousness are extremely impressive, are not sought out. And I have noticed the same trend in the other periodicals under consideration.

Why this neglect of contemporary Japanese poetry? Why the equation of "Japanese" with the courtly or Zen tradition of the distant past? Perhaps because modern, or rather postmodern Japan is too close to our own advanced capitalist world, too similar in its First World obsession with technology, urban and ecological problems, and so on. To put it another way, Japanese poetry—most of it in free verse and, like the poems above, in colloquial, up-to-date idiom—will not allow itself to be patronized; it is neither a poetry of victims nor of the oppressed, and it defines itself as a poetry very much of the present rather than of the historical imagination.

III

How Japanese, then, is Yasusada's lyric? And how does that lyric relate to our own late twentieth-century paradigms? Let me begin with the poem that so impressed Ron Silliman, "Telescope with Urn" from *Conjunctions*:

The image of the galaxies spreads out like a cloud of sperm.

Expanding said the observatory guide, and at such and such velocity.

It is like the idea of the flowers, opening within the idea of the flowers.

I like to think of that, said the monk, arranging them with his papery fingers.

Tiny were you, and squatted over a sky-colored bowl to make water.

What a big girl! cried we, tossing you in the general direction of the stars.

Intently, then, in the dream, I folded up the great telescope on Mount Horai.

In the form of this crane, it is small enough for the urn. (CON 69)

Compared to the Japanese poems I cited a moment ago, "Telescope with Urn" is elliptical and fragmentary. Each line, set off from the next by double spacing, is a separate sentence, and the sentences, while straightforward syntactically, tend not to connect. Reference, moreover, is often unclear as in "I like to think of that, said the monk, arranging them with his papery fingers," where we know neither what "that" is nor what "them" the monk is arranging. The poem's ellipsis is coupled with syn-

157

tactic inversion, as in "Tiny were you" and "What a big girl! cried we," with the Zen-like repetition of such phrases as "It is like the idea of the flowers, opening within the idea of the flowers," and with the circumlocution of "squatted over a sky-colored bowl to make water."

The effect of such devices is that the poem has a reassuringly "archaic," "oriental" feel; its reticence, dignity, and elusiveness, its references to Mount Horai, flowers, and stars bring to mind the ritual and stylization of Noh and Bunraku. At the same time, the "Japanese" nature imagery is eroticized in a distinctly modern way, and the "scientific" reference to the "velocity" of the expansion of the galaxies reminds us that this is an up-to-date lyric. And not just any up-to-date lyric but one about Hiroshima: "Telescope with Urn" refers to the death of the poet's young daughter in the nuclear raid. The urn with the crane on it is hers, and the poem contrasts the enormity of the macrocosm (the galaxies) with the terrifying microcosm of the life reduced to ashes inside the small urn.

Kent Johnson has thus found a perfect recipe for a new Orientalism, conceived in the best American tradition of Emerson's doctrine of "natural" hieroglyphic language, Pound's *Cathay*, and, most recently, Kenneth Rexroth's *Love Poems of Marichiko* (1978), presented by the poet as translations of the erotic lyrics of an actual Japanese woman although Rexroth later admitted he had made them up entirely himself.[15] The *Love Poems of Marichiko*, which Johnson surely knew, provided him with a blueprint for the fusion of concrete sexual imagery and "Buddhist" reticence.

But in the wake of the disjunctive poetry of the eighties and nineties, the demand is for greater obliquity, fragmentation, dislocation. For these, Johnson evidently turned to one of Rexroth's contemporaries, the Jack Spicer who produced the exotic *After Lorca*. Here is a sample:

> In the middle of my mirror
> A girl is drowning
> The voice of a single girl.
> She holds cold fire like a glass
> Each thing she watches
> Has become double.
> Cold fire is
> Cold fire is.
> In the middle of my mirror
> A girl is drowning
> The voice of a single girl.[16]

Spicer's poem is not as fragmented as Yasusada's but it has the same simple declarative sentences, the concrete imagery, the direct, naive tone, the delicate obliquity and ellipsis, as in "Cold fire is / Cold fire is." Like Spicer, Yasusada is obsessed by images of death, but, as Johnson has understood, in the post-Cold War era, there is little calling for the realistic descriptions of dismemberment favored by, say, Toge Sankichi. At the same time, Western guilt about the dropping of the bomb is such that the reader is programmed to find Yasusada's muted references to the Hiroshima "tragedy" moving, especially when these references are matter-of-fact and stoic.

"Telescope and Urn" thus satisfies our longing for a Japan, rather like that of Barthes's *Empire of Signs*, an imaginary Japan that is gentler and more dignified than the brash West, a world of grace, ritual, and transience, of elegant calligraphy and Zen gardens, a world in which the wrapping of packages is an art and chopsticks delicately separate bits of food, unlike those Western knives and forks which brutally cut up slices of meat. "It is like the idea of the flowers, opening within the idea of the flowers." Those delicate flowers, perhaps, that emerge from little paper balls dropped into a glass of water.

Consider another Yasusada poem, this one published in the little magazine *First Intensity* under the title "Mad Daughter and Big-Bang" and subtitled "December 25, 1945*", the mock footnote explaining that "In the aftermath of the bombing, many survivors moved into the hills, surrounding Hiroshima. This was the case with Yasusada and his daughter. —eds." [17]

> Walking in the vegetable patch
> late at night, I was startled to find
> the severed head of my
> mad daughter lying on the ground.
>
> Her eyes were upturned, gazing at me, ecstatic-like . . .
>
> (From a distance it had appeared
> to be a stone, haloed with light,
> as if cast there by the Big-Bang.)
>
> What on earth are you doing, I said,
> you look ridiculous.
>
> Some boys buried me here,
> she said sullenly.
>
> Her dark hair, comet-like, trailed behind . . .
>
> Squatting, I pulled the
> turnip up by the root.

Here the reference is again to the death of the poet's daughter in the Hiroshima raid. But the technique is somewhat different: for the elliptical and dislocated sentences of "Telescope and Urn," Johnson here substitutes narrative—a kind of "magic realist" narrative in which events are displaced and transformed. The hallucinatory presence of the dead child, transformed into a "mad daughter," the speech of the "severed head," the Maenad-like image of "dark hair, comet-like, trail[ing] behind," and the title's ironic allusion to "Big-Bang" theories—these give the poem the semblance of a dream, or rather a nightmare. At the same time, the daughter's "sullen" explanation that "Some boys buried me," is literally quite true if we take the "boys" to be the U.S. military. Again, in the poem's conclusion, the surreal image of "Squatting, I pulled the turnip up by the root," is accurate enough if we read it as a reference to the easy removal of the charred and rotten corpse from the ground in which the live body was "rooted." Such images play into the residual guilt of contemporary American readers, even as the poem's multiple ironies temper that guilt, allowing us to concentrate on the effectiveness of Johnson's fiction, especially the immediacy of the terse dialogue between father and daughter.

One would be hard put to find actual Hiroshima witness poems (or even later Japanese re-enactments of Hiroshima poems) that are characterized by such irony and restraint, such self-consciously surreal, oblique images. Rather, the matter-of-factness of the disconnected sentences, both here and elsewhere in the Yasusada manuscript, recalls such long prose poems as Ron Silliman's *Tjanting*. A Yasusada poem in *Grand Street* #53 (1995), for example, begins with the line "The sake shop hisses with its pleasures, all boiled up," and continues with such sentences as "Here is a black-haired man with a black-haired man," or "There are two sticks and a cup in Spring."[18] The relationship of these present-tense, simple declarative sentences to those that compose Japanese renga is taken up in a piece which was evidently Yasusada's American debut, the "tape-essay" called "Renga and the New Sentence," conducted in Madison, Wisconsin, December 1989, by Tosa Motokiyu, Ojiu Norinaga, and Okura Kyojin— the three familiar Yasusada translators-editors—and published in *Aerial*.[19] The dialogue takes up the issue of what Ron Silliman, in a well-known essay by that name, defined as "The New Sentence, " a "sentence" that is the building block of the new "poetic" prose, even as the line is the basic unit of the conventional poem.[20] Tosa Motokiyu and his collaborators cite Silliman's definition (see NS 91) verbatim:

1. The paragraph organizes the sentences;
2. The paragraph is a unit of quantity, not logic or argument;
3. Sentence length is a unit of measure;
4. Sentence structure is altered for torque, or increased polysemy / ambiguity;
5. Syllogistic movement is (a) limited; (b) controlled. . . . (AER 54)

Silliman, they note, claimed that the only precursor of the "New Sentence" was the William Carlos Williams of *Kora in Hell*, but, as they demonstrate, the "New Sentence" has a more significant source in "the Japanese haikai renga—a poetic form that anticipates by more than four centuries a number of the principles underlying 'new sentence' approaches to composition" (AER 52). As Motokiyu explains it, renga, like the "new sentence," is animated by "the faith that non-syllogistic movement may open onto alternate forms of perception" (AER 52). In twentieth-century experimental renga, moreover, "the stanzas shatter their prosodic constraints and move brazenly into prose," forcing "the written into new conceptual territory" (AER 52). And Kyojin cites Earl Miner's definition of renga in *Japanese Linked Verse*:

(T)he renga is no single thing. It has been practiced in short versions of two stanzas and in long versions up to ten thousand . . . (T)he art of linked poetry involves adding stanzas in such a fashion as to keep something but to change the meaning of what might be called the stanza itself and the stanza in connection with its predecessor. In such fashion the sequence is truly sequential and a sustained plot is impossible. (AER 52, ellipses are the author's).

Modes of linking, according to the translators, include "flat linking," "mosaic linking," "linking through paragram," "linking through assonances," and so on, all these devices "generating a prismatic and collective textuality" (AER 53). And they cite a traditional renga written by Matsuo Basho and Shita Yaba, which begins:

(MB) At a fragrance of plums, a blob, the sun, appears on a
    mountain path.
(SY) here and there a pheasant call rises
(SY) he begins repairing his house while there's nothing to do in
    spring
(MB) news from Kansai raises the price of rice
(MB) in the evening there was some pattering—now the moon
    among clouds
(SY) talking with a bush in between—the autumn, the loneliness
(AER 53)

The American Language poets now get a slight slap on the wrist because "they have not begun, really, to seriously move outside the ideologically constructed parameters of single-author composition"; indeed, with rare exceptions like "Legend" (written by Bruce Andrews, Charles Bernstein, Ray Di Palma, Steve McCaffery and Ron Silliman), they have insisted on "self attribution" and "personal ownership" of texts" (AER 55). They should, according to our Japanese discussants, experiment more fully with depersonalized Buddhist sensibilities, should eschew ownership of their verse. And now we are introduced to a renga by three Hiroshima poets: Araki Yasusada, Ozaki Kusatao, and Akutagawa Fusei.

This renga, ostensibly of the 1930s, is introduced by a defensive letter of June, 1937, from Yasusada to Ogiwara Seisensui, the head of the *Soun* avant-garde group. Yasusada defends the "impure" linking used in their renga and argues that "*dissonance*" is its "deep measure." A footnote on the part of the translators tells us that this letter is "Among the over 100 carbon copies of Yasusada's letters in our possession. It is interesting that Yasusada and his friends were very influenced by the American poet Jack Spicer; indeed, a few of their renga are dedicated to him" (AER 59). And they insert another letter, this one to Fusei, dated November 17, 1965, in which Yasusada describes his enthusiasm for the "new" California poets whose books his friend Natsume Kuribayashi has brought to Hiroshima: Robert Duncan, Alex [sic] Ginsberg, John Wieners, Brother Antoninus, Philip Lamantia, and especially Jack Spicer, whose *Billy the Kid*, and *Heads of the Town Up to the Aether* are declared to be kindred works.[21]

There are a number of incongruous details here. Why, to begin with, would such "experts" as Tosa Motokiyu and his friends rely on the American scholar Earl Miner's definition of renga? And how could the footnote to the 1937 letter refer to the Spicer influence, Spicer then being twelve years old! Neither the editor of *Aerial* nor the journal's readers seem to have been bothered by these lacunae, evidently because the affiliation of the "new" Language poetry with the "old" renga seemed so appealing, giving Silliman's own poems a new authority. Here are the first nine lines of the renga itself:

Happening to notice the willow leaves in the garden, a braille page of words

The voices of the sorority girls sing of fucking in a plaintive way

Dressing their frail bodies in armor are the young widows of the prefecture of

It was there we saw the trace ruins of an ancient dog-shooting range

So running after me was the young child whose name is Manifold

A screen of moonflowers and creeping gourds, with a thicket of cockscomb and goosefoot, evoking cocks and cunts

She told me that the master of the house had left for a certain location in town and that I had better look for him there pronto, if I desired to speak to him

Everybody was fucking overjoyed to see him, as if he had returned from the dead

Terrified by these words he walked straight into the province of Kaga

(AER 57-58)

The translator Okura Kyojin comments: "Similarities with 'new sentence' writing seem compelling. The hokku unit is now extended out into pure prose utterance. As Fusei says elsewhere: 'no easy messages, no intention to share self-emotion; no lyrical intensity—percussive soundings within patterns of harmonic and dissonant chords. Utterance as autonomous fact *and* its saturation in context. *This* tension. Gaps now as intrinsic to such grammar . . .'" (AER 58, ellipses' the author's).

What could sound more contemporary, more late twentieth-century American than the frank sexual references to the "sorority girls" who "sing of fucking," and to "cocks and cunts" as well as to the slang of "Everybody was fucking overjoyed" or "I had better look for him there pronto." And yet all the Japanese properties are here: the "willow leaves in the garden," the "screen of moonflowers and creeping gourds," the "master of the house," the young girls' "frail bodies" the "province of Kaga." The layering of language registers reminds me of nothing so much as Pound's *Electra*, where the poet brings Sophocles' great tragedy into his own post-World War II orbit (the play was written with Rudd Flemming while Pound was incarcerated in St. Elizabeth's) by juxtaposing lines of the original Greek (especially in Electra's speeches) to the Western twang of Orestes' revenge speech:

> This is what we're agoin' to do,
> listen sharp and check up if
> I miss any bullseyes . . .
> you nip into this building, find out everything that's
> being done there, and keep us wise to the lot of it. Snap.

or the flat vulgarities of Clytemnestra, here presented as a vindictive shrew:

> You've shot off a lot of brash talk
> to a lot of people,
> a lot more than was so
> about how forward I am, how unjust
> insulting you and your gang.[22]

In thus deconstructing the expected linguistic registers, Pound found a way of relating Electra's ancient tragedy to his own situation as a condemned war traitor.

In inventing a Japan to satisfy contemporary American fantasies as to a less complicated, more orderly society—a society at once highly refined and yet quite frank about sexuality — Johnson uses one other form of layering that deserves mention. In all the Yasusada portfolios published to date, the poems are embedded in a larger archive, that consists of letters, English assignments (see APR 25), commentaries, and elaborate footnotes. The model would be the palimpsestic notebooks of George Oppen, where drafts of poems are surrounded by extracts from Heidegger and other philosophers, by letters, autobiographical notes, source material, and so on.[23] Clearly, contemporary readers have a predilection for this sort of documentary material. Yasusada, telling Kusatao in April, 1965, that he has been in the hospital for a "couple stays" (would any Japanese translator use this slang expression?), informs his friend that "The difficulty, as you know, is the sickness after treatment." "Luckily," Yasusada adds, "the hospital wing they have me in looks out on the pine-covered hills of Mount Asano" (APR 25). How authentic! How vivid! What a reminder of the Hiroshima tragedy! And Yasusada has an English teacher, Mr. Rogers, who advises him to study the writer James Joyce, "who is famous for a form of writing called 'streams [sic] of consciousness'" (APR 25). Again, how quaint and charmingly incorrect, at least when we don't probe too carefully into the conundrum that Yasusada might not know Joyce although he does know Spicer.

IV

Kent Johnson has, I think, done a brilliant job in inventing a world at once ritualized and yet startlingly modern, timeless yet documentary, archaicized yet *au courant*—a poetic world that satisfies our hunger for the *authentic*, even though that authentic is itself a simulacrum. To call his Yasusada impersonation a hoax, much less a "criminal act", is of course absurd: the pseudonym is a time-honored device in literature, and from James McPherson's *Ossian* to the present, writers have invented fictional personae and passed them off as the real thing.

Still, there is something deeply troubling about the uncritical reception of these "Japanese" poems and prose pieces, with their brash distortions of literary and political history and their questionable conjunctions of jarring verbal registers. Why is it, one wonders, that none of Yasusada's editors sought out the guidance of bona fide Japanese poets, scholars, or translators? That they didn't read these "newly found" and never before published works against the well-known brilliant poetries of, say, Tanikawa Shuntaro? And that, once exposed as having been "taken in" by the "hoax", they have put the blame on everyone but themselves? Let me try to summarize the reasons why the "hoax" has worked so well, and why, so I believe, similar inventions will occur with increasing frequency as we move toward the millenium.

First, most academics today (and most poets and editors, after all, now hold academic posts) pay lip service to the Foucaultian notion of cultural construction, of discourse networks that discipline the individual talent. Hence the search for novel and interesting cultural positioning, as in the case of Araki Yasusada, that rare Hiroshima survivor to have turned up so conveniently so late in the day, with such a fascinating cache of never-before-published poems and documents. Never mind Araki Yasusada the individual: it is his identitarian self that matters, his occupation of the position of avant-gardist who is also victim, disseminator of Jack Spicer, Roland Barthes, and the Language poets, who is also a traditional renga and haiku poet, purveyor of dissonant chords and gaps in grammar who also has something centrally important to say about atomic warfare, and quintessential neglected genius who is also a communitarian, believing that there is no such thing as "ownership" of one's writings.

Yasusada thus satisfies, as fully as possible, the current disciplinary demand. Yet, despite the continuing predilection for viewing individual poetry as the fruit of such cultural construction, there is another demand, this one deep-seated and instinctive, for individual authenticity, for uniqueness, for the Benjaminian aura that comes only in the presence of the Real Thing, not its copies. Look at that letter written from the Hiroshima hospital in 1965! Look at the elegiac lines written to a particular wife and daughter! Look at the correspondence with his very own English teacher and the mistakes that Yasusada makes in his assignments, misspelling words like "him" ("Hime"), "sky" ("skye") and "patrolling" ("patroleling") in ways, so my Japanese sources tell me, no Japanese student of English who was as far along as Yasusada, would possibly make. These ancillary documents, in any case, humanize the situation; they give Yasusada a particular habitation and a name and make his work more accessible for the readers of *American Poetry Review* or *Grand Street*.

Accessibility, in this case, has much to do with the paradox that even as Yasusada's poetry satisfies an American reader's demand, his work *makes no demand on us*. We can empathize with the "tragedy" in which Yasusada was caught up in the prime of his life (he was thirty-eight at the time of the nuclear attack), without having to think through the ethical issues involved in any serious way. The Yasusada archive puts forward no choice we would have to make, triggers no moral or psychological debate we might engage in. Rather, the work's mode is, as I remarked earlier, Orientalism, "that Western style," in Edward Said's words, "for dominating, restructuring, and having authority over the Orient— an Orient represented since antiquity as "a place of romance, exotic beings, haunting memories and landscapes, remarkable experiences."[24] And the great irony of the current situation in American letters is that the New Multiculturalism, far from countering the Orientalism Said decried as long as twenty years ago, has turned out to be its inadvertent promoter.

How did we get ourselves into this bind? Partly, no doubt, because our current skepticism, indeed cynicism, as to the power and efficacy of government (that is, *our* government) is generally coupled with an uncritical—or at least unquestioning—attitude toward the governments of other nations. The Cold War, as it is currently represented in the literary and visual arts, is almost invariably *our* Cold War, the bombing of Hiroshima, *our* infamy. The complexities and contradictions of geopolitics thus take a back seat to moral outrage on the one hand, fictional construction on the other.

In forcing us to think about these questions, Kent Johnson has performed an invaluable service. His Yasusada manuscript challenges many dubious notions: for example, that the "new sentence," as conceived by Ron Silliman and his friends, has no precedent in poetry, that certain "tragic" events cannot be the "subject" of surreal or parodic treatment, and that literary influence (Spicer and Barthes on Yasusada) exists if and when the influenced author claims it does. Like Pound's *Homage to Sextus Propertius*, the Yasusada notebooks force us to go back to the "originals," so as to see what they really were and how they have been transformed. One can argue, of course, that Pound did write *Propertius* in his own name; he did not, as Johnson does, pose as someone else. But the fact is that Pound was already famous when he wrote his Latin "translation" and so he could afford to be Ezra Pound, whereas the unknown Kent Johnson, writing in what is an increasingly glutted and cut-throat poetry market, had no such alternative. Johnson took, in other words, the *Ossian* route rather than the route of Pound or of the Goethe of the *West-Oestlicher Divan*. But just as McPherson's *Ossian* brought on a valuable reconsideration of the *medieval*, so "Yasusada" may prompt us to familiarize ourselves with the actual Hiroshima memoirs of the fifties and sixties, as well as with Japanese postwar poetry in its specific articulations. What we need are not more "authentic" and "sensitive" witnesses to what we take to be exotic cultural and ethnic practices, but a willingness, on the part of poet as well as reader, to look searchingly and critically at what is always already *there*.

FOOTNOTES

1 "Doubled Flowering: From the Notebooks of Araki Yasusada," translated by Tosa Motokiyu, Okura Kyojin, and Ojiu Noringa: A Special Supplement," *American Poetry Review* 25, no. 4 (July / August 1996): 23-26, p. 23. Subsequent references in the text cited as APR.

2 Araki Yasusada, "Telescope with Urn," *Conjunctions 23: New World Writing* (Autumn 1994:): 69. Subsequently cited as CON.

3 Ron Silliman, posting to Buffalo Poetics List (POETICS@LISTSERV.ACSU.BUF-FALO.EDU), 21 December 1994.

4 Emily Nussbaum, "Turning Japanese: The Hiroshima Poetry Hoax," *Lingua Franca*, November 1996): 82. Subsequently cited in the text as LF. In the September/October issue of *American Poetry Review*, the editors published a recension of the Yasusada "Special Supplement," and apologized to their readership for the fraud.

5 I owe this and subsequent bits of information about Japanese usage to Dr. Akitoshi Nagahata of Nagoya University.

6 Seisensui is a real haiku master, although again the name is reversed; the family name is Ogiwara.

7 See Hugh Kenner, *The Pound Era* (Berkeley and Los Angeles: University of

California Press, 1971), p. 207. The passage transcribes the Chinese poem "The Unmoving Cloud" by To-Em-Mei.

8   Ezra Pound, "Homage to Sextus Propertius," in *Personae: The Shorter Poems of Ezra Pound*, rev. ed. by Lea Baechler and A. Walton Litz (New York: New Directions, 1990), p. 206.

9   In conversation, Rod Smith has told me that he suspected all along the manuscript he received was a hoax but he found it so charming and apropos he decided to publish it.

10 Michael Foucault, "What Is an Author?" (1969), in Foucault, *Language, Counter-Memory, Practice*: Selected Essays and Interviews, ed. Donald F. Bouchard, trans. Donald F. Bouchard and Sherry Simon (Ithaca: Cornell University Press, 1977), pp. 113-38, see p. 116. Subsequently cited as MF.

11 Jiro Nakano (ed. and trans.), *Outcry from the Inferno: Atomic Bomb Tanka Anthology*, Special Double issue of *Bamboo Ridge, The Hawaii Writers Quarterly*, issues #67 and #68 (Honolulu, Summer/Fall 1995). Subsequently cited as OI. According to Earl Miner, *The New Princeton Encyclopedia of Poetry and Poetics*, ed. Alex Preminger and T. V. F. Brogan (Princeton: Princeton University Press, 1993),p. 1265: "*Tanka* is a Japanese form originating in the 7th century which consists of 31 morae (conventionally construed syllables) in lines of 5, 7, 5, 7, and 7. Hypersyllabic but not hyposyllabic lines are allowed." "It is," says Miner, "the definitive literary form in Japanese poetry."
For an American version of the poetry of the Hiroshima experience, see Marc Kaminsky, *Road from Hiroshima* (New York: Simon and Schuster, 1984). Kaminsky's lyrics are based on testimony of survivors of Hiroshima and Nagasaki; the author calls them "collages in which the actual and the imaginary freely mix" (p. 111). A typical poem, "The Shopkeeper's Assistant," begins:

> It happened something like an electric short
> a bluish-white light
> blanked out everything. . . . (p. 41)

12 Richard H. Minear (ed. and trans.), *Hiroshima: Three Witnesses* (Princeton: Princeton University Press, 1990). Subsequently cited as HTW.

13 See "Four Poems from Hiroshima: selected and with an introduction by Tsuneko Yoshikawa, trans. Steven Forth," *American Poetry Review* (July/August 1985): 8-10. An interesting recent Hiroshima memoir is Hideko Tamura Snider's *One Sunny Day: A Child's Memories of Hiroshima*, foreword by Studs Terkel (Chicago and LaSalle: Open Court, 1996). Tamura Snider was ten years old the day of the attack and her account of the devastation is very vivid and moving. But for her and her characteristically apolitical family (a family living at a time when the government ruled by decree and there were no opposition parties), Hiroshima essentially meant the loss of one's nearest and dearest (Hideko Tamura lost her mother), and how the populace coped with that loss. The issues are not construed as "political."

14 Leith Morton (ed. and trans.), *An Anthology of Contemporary Japanese Poetry* (New York and London: Garland, 1993). Subsequently cited in the text as LM. Another excellent anthology is *Modern Japanese Poetry*, trans. James Kirkup, ed. A. R. Davis (St. Lucia, Queensland: University of Queensland Press, 1978). Kirkup's range is wider than Morton's—he includes eighty-three poets as compared to Morton's sixteen—but thematically, tonally, and prosodically, the poems are quite

similar. Here, for example, is "My Body" by Takahashi Shinkichi (b. 1901):

I have been broken into pieces:
those green leaves thick on the persimmon tree
are my hands and feet rustling in the wind.

That bright-coloured butterfly fluttering by
has my eyes in those spots on her wings.

The future is surrounded by
a moving wall of earth.

A dog is pregnant with the earth,
the gods sucking its pointed nipples.

Each nipple is as big as the point on a red pencil.

I have been swimming in fire and water.
A plane has flown between my straddled legs.
The sky is my body. (p. 84)

15 See Robert Kern's excellent *Orientalism, Modernism, and the American Poem* (Cambridge and New York: Cambridge University Press, 1996). The *Love Poems of Marichiko* will be found in Rexroth's *The Morning Star* (New York: New Directions, 1979), pp. 47-82.

    The classic discussion of orientalism as a Western discourse is, of course, Edward Said's in *Orientalism* (New York: Random House, 1978).

16 Jack Spicer, "Song of Two Windows," *After Lorca* (1957), in *The Collected Books of Jack Spicer*, ed. & with a Commentary by Robin Blaser (Los Angeles: Black Sparrow Press, 1975), pp. 46-47.

17 Araki Yasusada, "Mad Daughter and Big Bang," *First Intensity* #5 (1996), p. 10.

18 "Untitled: August 12, 1964," *Grand Street*, 53 (1995), p. 25.

19 See Tosa Motokiyu, Ojiu Norinaga, and Okura Kyojin, "Renga and the New Sentence," *Aerial* 6/7 (Washington, D.C.: Edge Books, 1991): 52-59. Subsequently cited in the text as AER.

20 The essay was originally published in *Talks: Hills* 6/7 (1980): 190-217, and is reprinted in Ron Silliman, *The New Sentence* (New York: Roof, 1987), pp. 63-93. Subsequently cited in the text as NS.

21 AER 59. Note that this list overlaps with that in the November 7 letter, also to Fusei, reproduced in APR 26; see p. 5 above.

22 Sophocles, *Electra*, a Version by Ezra Pound and Rudd Fleming, with an Introduction and Production Notes by Carey Perloff (New York: New Directions, 1990), pp. 4, 23. See Carey Perloff's commentary on the complexities of language, pp. ix-xxv.

23 On the "palimpsestic" text as quintessentially postmodern, see Michael Davidson, "Palimtexts: Postmodern Poetry and the Material Text," in *Postmodern Genres*, ed. Marjorie Perloff (Norman: University of Oklahoma Press, 1989), pp. 75-95.

24 Edward Said, *Orientalism*, pp. 3, 1.

ROOF BOOKS (Partial List)

Andrews, Bruce. **EX WHY ZEE.** 112p. $10.95.
Andrews, Bruce. **Getting Ready To Have Been Frightened**. 116p. $7.50.
Benson, Steve. **Blue Book**. Copub. with The Figures. 250p. $12.50
Bernstein, Charles. **Islets/Irritations**. 112p. $9.95.
Bernstein, Charles (editor). **The Politics of Poetic Form**. 246p. $12.95; cloth $21.95.
Brossard, Nicole. **Picture Theory**. 188p. $11.95.
Child, Abigail. **Scatter Matrix**. 79p. $9.95.
Davies, Alan. **Active 24 Hours**. 100p. $5.
Davies, Alan. **Signage**. 184p. $11.
Davies, Alan. **Rave**. 64p. $7.95.
Day, Jean. **A Young Recruit**. 58p. $6.
Di Palma, Ray. **Motion of the Cypher**. 112p. $10.95.
Di Palma, Ray. **Raik**. 100p. $9.95.
Doris, Stacy. **Kildare**. 104p. $9.95.
Dreyer, Lynne. **The White Museum**. 80p. $6.
Edwards, Ken. **Good Science**. 80p. $9.95.
Eigner, Larry. **Areas Lights Heights**. 182p. $12, $22 (cloth).
Gizzi, Michael. **Continental Harmonies**. 92p. $8.95.
Gottlieb, Michael. **Ninety-Six Tears**. 88p. $5.
Grenier, Robert. **A Day at the Beach**. 80p. $6.
Grosman, Ernesto. **The XUL Reader: An Anthology of Argentine Poetry (1981–1996)**.
    167p. $14.95.
Hills, Henry. **Making Money**. 72p. $7.50. VHS videotape $24.95. Book & tape $29.95.
Huang, Yunte. **SHI: A Radical Reading of Chinese Poetry.** 76 p. $9.95.
Hunt, Erica. **Local History**. 80 p. $9.95.
Inman, P. **Criss Cross**. 64 p. $7.95.
Inman, P. **Red Shift**. 64p. $6.
Lazer, Hank. **Doublespace**. 192 p. $12.
Mac Low, Jackson. **Representative Works: 1938–1985**. 360p. $12.95, $18.95 (cloth).
Mac Low, Jackson. **Twenties**. 112p. $8.95.
Moriarty, Laura. **Rondeaux**. 107p. $8.
Neilson, Melanie. **Civil Noir**. 96p. $8.95.
Pearson, Ted. **Planetary Gear**. 72p. $8.95.
Perelman, Bob. **Virtual Reality**. 80p. $9.95.
Piombino, Nick, **The Boundary of Blur**. 128p. $13.95.
Raworth, Tom. **Clean & Will-Lit**. 106p. $10.95.
Robinson, Kit. **Balance Sheet**. 112p. $9.95.
Robinson, Kit. **Ice Cubes**. 96p. $6.
Scalapino, Leslie. **Objects in the Terrifying Tense Longing from Taking Place**. 88p. $9.95.
Seaton, Peter. **The Son Master**. 64p. $5.
Sherry, James. **Popular Fiction**. 84p. $6.
Silliman, Ron. **The New Sentence**. 200p. $10.
Silliman, Ron. **N/O**. 112p. $10.95.
Templeton, Fiona. **Cells of Release**. 128p. with photographs. $13.95.
Templeton, Fiona. **YOU—The City**. 150p. $11.95.
Ward, Diane. **Human Ceiling**. 80p. $8.95.
Ward, Diane. **Relation**. 64p. $7.50.
Watten, Barrett. **Progress**. 122p. $7.50.
Weiner, Hannah. **We Speak Silent**. 76 p. $9.95